Sonrise Stable
Operation Christmas Spirit

Vicki Watson

Illustrated by
Janet Griffin-Scott

The questions in the back of the book may be discussed after reading each chapter.

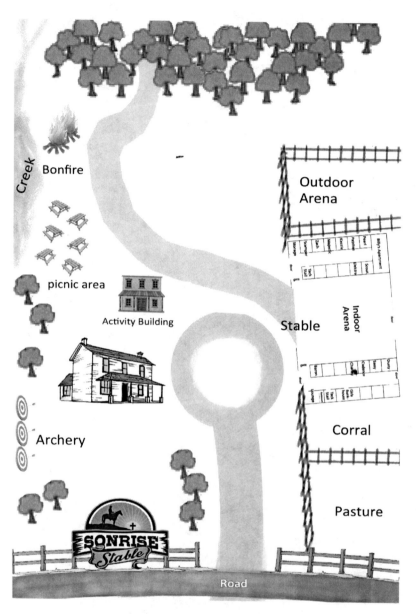

Sonrise Stable Map

Introduction to the Characters

Twelve-year-old **Rosie** and her adopted sister, **Carrie**, live with their parents, **Kristy** and **Eric Jackson**, and their maternal grandmother on one hundred acres at Sonrise Stable. Kristy has two sisters, Julie and Lisa—Rosie and Carrie's aunts.

Julie, Jonathan, and their son **Jared**, along with twins **Jamie** and **Jessie**, live two miles from Sonrise Stable.

Lisa, Robert, and their daughter, **Lauren**, recently moved from Texas to a log cabin at the back of the Sonrise Stable property.

The children are all homeschooled and help run the summer camps. They take care of their own horses as well as the horses boarded at the stable. Rosie's horse is Scamper and Carrie's is Zach. Both girls recently participated in a 4-H competitive trail ride.

Billy, a Sonrise Stable employee, is nineteen and lives in an apartment at the back of the barn. He owns a mule named Sassy.

Abigail Miller is a thirteen-year-old girl who boards her Arabian horse, Raja, at Sonrise Stable. She was Rosie's rival in the trail ride.

1
The Auction

How about this one?" Rosie led the way to the next pen at the livestock auction barn. Carrie, Lauren, and their grandmother followed her. When Rosie reached into the stall to pet the dark bay gelding, he snorted and jumped back, showing the whites of his eyes. She studied the horse, concerned that he had retreated to the back of the pen. His eyes were riveted on her.

Carrie and Lauren walked up on either side of Rosie, put their hands on the stall boards, and peeked through.

Rosie spoke to her grandmother but kept her eyes on the gelding. "Why is he so afraid?"

"Sometimes horses brought to these sales have been abused," Grandma said, "but maybe he's just nervous. It's a new place, and there's a lot going on."

They were walking down the outside of the long barn looking at horses in the outer pens. There certainly was a lot going on. The auction would begin at eleven, not for another hour. People continued to bring tack and equipment as well as animals to sell.

"Could we find a horse for me here?" Lauren asked.

Grandma glanced at the gelding cowering in the back of the stall and frowned. "I don't think so."

"Aw, Grandma. Why not? We haven't seen that many yet. There might be a good one here."

Lauren had what Grandma called "horse fever." Rosie remembered suffering from that same disease before Scamper was born. As far as she knew, the only cure for it was to get a horse of your own. But Rosie also understood her grandmother's hesitation. Although it felt bad not to have a horse, having the wrong one was even worse. Since Lauren wasn't an experienced rider, it was important that her first horse be gentle and safe.

Grandma sometimes said, "Green horse plus green rider equals black and blue." Rosie didn't want Lauren to get hurt on a horse that wasn't well-trained.

Carrie leaned forward and spoke softly, trying to coax the gelding to come to her, but he turned his head away.

The sounds of the horses around them filled the air. Normally Rosie loved to hear horses whinnying, but this was different. The horses calling to each other sounded frightened. It made her feel sad. Many of them were here because no one wanted them. She wished she had enough money to buy them all and give them a home for the rest of their lives where they would be safe and well cared for.

"We're here to buy a pony," Grandma reminded them, "not a horse."

Lauren sighed. "I know."

Their pony, Charley, would be excited if they brought a little friend home for him. Grandma planned to help the girls train Charley to pull a cart. Because he was so small, they hoped to find another his size. Eventually they wanted a team of ponies in order to give wagon rides around Sonrise Stable.

Suddenly there was a commotion in the parking lot behind them—a whinnying that was louder and more frantic than the rest. Rosie whirled around and saw a tall chestnut backing rapidly out of a stock trailer. The horse reared and yanked the lead rope from his owner's hand.

Before the animal had a chance to run away, an Amish boy darted from the barn toward the trailer and grabbed the rope. The boy stood still and patted the horse's neck. His quiet, gentle approach calmed the horse.

Rosie noticed a whole row of Amish buggies at one end of the parking lot with their horses tied to a rail. She felt drawn toward them like a magnet. Grandma seemed to understand and followed her.

First in the line was a small pony hooked to a cart. Rosie thought all ponies were cute, but this chubby palomino was especially so, standing next to the bigger horses as if he were one of them. Seeing the pony made Rosie more excited about someday driving her own.

The horses stamped their hooves and bit at their sides to chase away the pesky flies. Late September in Ohio brought challenging weather for horses. Their winter coats were growing, but the daytime temperatures were sometimes, like today, as warm as midsummer. As she walked down the line, she noticed that the long fur on the buggy horses' necks was wavy with dried sweat.

Rosie figured the horses were as uncomfortable as she would be if she ran a mile in her winter coat on a warm day. She wondered why they didn't have any water. There wasn't a bucket or water trough in sight.

This wasn't the first time Rosie had seen the Amish. Occasionally they drove their buggies down the country road that ran in front of Sonrise Stable.

There were many Amish men and boys at the sale today. The men all had long beards. The boys had bowl-shaped haircuts and wore blue pants with suspenders and light blue, button-down shirts.

Rosie turned her attention back to the tall, lean horse that had nearly escaped. "He looks like a Thoroughbred."

"Could be." Grandma led the girls to a line of trailers with sale items. "Many Thoroughbreds and Standardbreds end up here."

"You mean there are racehorses here?" Lauren asked.

"The ones that are too slow to race are sent here from the tracks and training stables. Even some that have had successful racing careers may be sold once they get too old to run."

That wasn't fair. Rosie frowned. Why would a good racehorse be sold at an auction like this? She was beginning to wish she hadn't come with her grandmother today.

"The Amish buy many of the Standardbreds, harness-racing horses, to pull their buggies. They're trained to drive—and they're fast." Grandma nodded toward the Amish boy who had caught the horse. "He'll have his own buggy in a few years and will want a nice, fast horse to pull it."

Rosie wondered what it was like to travel everywhere in a buggy rather than a car. It must be fun to live on an Amish farm—unless of course the girls weren't allowed to ride horses. She wouldn't like that.

The Amish boys laughed and played together. A couple of the younger ones sat on the ground digging in the dirt with sticks. Soon she would have a little brother—Gabriel. He'd probably dig in the dirt someday too. Her mom was at home getting the house ready for another inspection by the foster agency. There were so many things to do before Gabe's arrival. Rosie couldn't wait to be a big sister. Well, technically she already was. Carrie was her little sister, but only by a few months so that didn't count.

4

There weren't many boys in the family. In fact, just one—Rosie's cousin Jared. There was Billy too. He was nineteen and worked at the stable. Although he wasn't related, Billy was around so much she sometimes forgot he wasn't a member of the family. Rosie wanted to teach her little brother how to ride Charley. The scraggly little pony would be perfect for Gabe's first horse. Of course, she'd have to wait a while since the boy was only three months old.

Rows of trucks and trailers filled the parking lot. Most of the people had items to sell displayed next to their rigs. Grandma stopped at a silver trailer where several pony carts stood on end, shafts pointing straight up in the air. She took hold of the first one and pulled down on the shaft until the cart was in the driving position.

Grandma wasn't going to buy that old thing, was she? The beat-up cart wasn't at all what Rosie had imagined they'd use for driving the ponies. It looked as if it had been through a war. She pointed to the cart. "It doesn't have a seat!"

"Did you think I didn't notice that?" Her grandmother stepped between the shafts where the pony would be and pulled it a few steps.

"We don't need a pony," Lauren laughed. "Grandma could give everyone rides!"

Grandma shook her head. "I'll leave that to Charley and the pony we buy today."

Rosie hoped they would find one today that her grandmother approved of. After the camps that summer, Grandma had become more particular about the type of horse she was willing to buy. Rosie ran her hand over the metal frame of the cart. The chipped gray paint on the shafts felt rough against her fingertips. She nodded toward the next trailer. "What about that one over there, with two seats and the big wooden wheels?"

"That's a beautiful cart, but I'm sure it has a price tag to go with it." Grandma rolled the old cart back into place and set it up on end.

"This one isn't too bad. I'll bet your dad or Billy could add a seat, and with some sanding and a paint job have it looking almost like new."

Rosie wasn't so sure about that, but she supposed an ugly cart was better than no cart at all. She moved on and looked at the other items for sale. "We need some harness too." Rosie picked up a stiff, moldy leather strap from a pile on the ground and wrinkled her nose at the musty smell. If only she had enough money, she'd buy a brand-new set of harness.

Grandma wrinkled her nose at the harness too. "Hmm. It might be all right, but it's covered in so much mold it's hard to see the leather." She examined the other two carts and then said, "Let's go, girls."

"Aren't you going to buy anything?" Carrie asked.

"Maybe," Grandma said. "But I won't know what size cart or harness we need until we find a pony. Haven't you heard the expression 'Don't put the cart before the horse'?"

"But we're not buying a horse," Lauren said.

"Okay then, let's not put the cart before the pony," Grandma laughed. "If we get a pony, and if I have enough money left, we'll come back to see whether the carts and harness are still here. They're in such bad shape; we won't have too much competition for them."

The girls raced back to the barn. Rosie had never seen such a variety of horses in one place—everything from cow-hocked miniatures with long, shaggy manes and potbellies to huge, tired-looking draft horses with hooves the size of dinner plates.

They continued down the row of animals for sale. Every time the girls thought they had located the right pony, their grandmother managed to find something wrong with it—too mean, too timid, too old, too young, foundered, sick, or injured.

Rosie was about ready to give up when she spotted a shaggy head peeking out of a pen ahead of them. "Grandma, over there! That one looks exactly like Charley!"

2
Rascal

As they approached, the chestnut pony didn't back up fearfully. Instead, he tilted his head oddly and watched them. Two Amish boys inside the pen were tying a hay bag to one of the rails.

"Hello, boys." Grandma walked over and patted the pony. "Who do we have here?"

The shorter boy piped up. "Rascal."

The older boy elbowed him and shook his head. "Sorry, he's mixed up. This is Jeremiah."

The boy spoke to the younger one in a different language. Even though she knew it wasn't polite, Rosie stared at them. He seemed to talk much faster than normal. She couldn't understand a word he said.

He resumed speaking in English. "My name is Daniel." He put his hand on the smaller one's shoulder. "And this is my little brother, Reuben."

Even when Daniel spoke English, it sounded different to Rosie. She couldn't have said exactly what the difference was, but he didn't say the words the same way she did.

"Hi. I'm Rosie." She started to introduce the boys to her family but stopped when she noticed her grandmother moving her index finger toward the pony's eye. "Grandma, what are you doing?"

Her grandmother's finger continued moving closer until the pony blinked and tossed his head. "Checking his eyesight. The way he tilted his head earlier made me wonder. Horses often do that when they can't see well." She repeated the finger test on the other side, and this time the pony responded more quickly. She patted his shoulder. "I guess your vision is all right. Rosie, why don't you check his teeth and tell me how old you think he is?"

"Okay," Rosie said. "Carrie, would you hold him for me?"

Daniel opened the gate to the pen, and the girls stepped inside.

Carrie moved to the right of the pony and put a halter on his head. Rosie had learned how to do this in 4-H. She slipped her thumb and finger into Rascal's mouth, at the back where he didn't have any teeth. Grandma stood beside her and watched.

It was easy to tell the age when she was looking at pictures in a book, but on a real horse, it was difficult—especially on this fidgety pony, who kept moving around, and opening and closing his mouth. Rosie could barely see his teeth at all.

Finally, she let go of the pony's mouth and wiped her hands on her jeans. "Hmm. I'd say about five or six."

Grandma nodded. "That sounds right. He has all his permanent teeth, but they're not worn yet."

"Is he trained to pull a cart?" Lauren asked.

Reuben began to shake his head, but Daniel elbowed him again and spoke a few sharp words in the other language. The younger boy climbed out of the pen and sat cross-legged on the ground.

Daniel stroked the pony's neck. "Yes. My younger brothers drive him to school."

"You're allowed to drive a pony to school?" Of course, since Rosie was homeschooled, she could drive Charley to her school too, but going from the barn to the house wasn't as exciting as driving down the road to an actual school building. "How many brothers do you have?"

Daniel thought for a moment as if he were counting them in his head. "Eight brothers—and three sisters."

"Wow!" Rosie wondered if all eight boys rode in the cart at once. She was excited about getting a new brother. That would give her one brother and one sister. Having eleven siblings was beyond her comprehension. Counting all her cousins, there were only six kids in their entire family.

Grandma reached for the lead rope. "Can we take him out?"

"Yes ma'am." Daniel handed Grandma the lead and opened the gate. She led the pony away from the pens, stopped and backed him, then picked up each hoof.

Rascal had the same chestnut coat and shaggy mane as Charley. They were nearly identical, except Rascal had a long blaze that extended down to his muzzle. Rosie noticed a tag stuck on top of the pony's hindquarters with the number thirty-five, indicating his order in the sale. She felt a strange connection to this pony that looked like

Charley's twin. Would her grandmother find something wrong with him as she had all the others?

Grandma stared at the pony for a while, absentmindedly rubbing his ears, then handed his lead rope back to the boy. "Thank you, Daniel." She started walking toward the next pen. "Let's keep going, girls."

"Aren't we going to get him?" Rosie couldn't believe her grandmother wasn't ready to buy the pony. "Is there something wrong with him too?"

When they were out of earshot of the Amish boys, Grandma said, "I studied German years ago in college. The Amish speak a variation of that called Pennsylvania Dutch. While I couldn't understand everything the older boy said, I picked up enough to guess that Rascal probably earned that name for a good reason."

"What do you mean?" Lauren asked.

Carrie nodded. "I noticed that every time Reuben tried to say something, Daniel stopped him."

"From what I understood, this pony has never been driven."

Rosie stuffed her hands deep into her front pockets. "But the boy said…"

Grandma shook her head. "Not everyone is honest—especially when it comes to selling horses."

Rosie knew that was true. She remembered when they bought Charley. They had actually gone to look at a mare, Tilly, that was advertised in a newspaper. She had turned out to be quite wild— nothing at all like she was described in the ad. "But those boys are Amish. Aren't Amish people always honest?"

"They're human," Grandma stated. "Come on. Let's see what else is here."

Grandma walked into the barn and led the way to a set of rough wooden stairs. They climbed to a walkway, which passed over a group of large pens that held more horses of all different colors

10

and sizes. Some were eating hay. Others whinnied or milled about restlessly.

"Look at those two over there." Rosie pointed out two light-colored mares, in the pen below. They stood head to tail with their heads resting on top of each other's backs.

Grandma walked over and stood beside Rosie.

"Aren't they beautiful?" Rosie said. "Do you think they're sisters?"

"They might be, the way they're protecting each other," Grandma said. "Cremellos. That's a color you don't see too often."

They were at the sale to buy a pony, but the two mares seemed so sweet. With enough training, they could be used at Sonrise Stable. Rosie thought it was worth a try. "Do you think we could buy them?"

Grandma shook her head sadly. "I love how they're watching out for each other, but we can't buy them all. Every horse we take home requires vet and farrier care—and lots of food. You know it's expensive to own a horse."

"But those two seem so special."

"Yes, they do, but they're young, maybe yearlings. Billy's already training your colt. We raised Majestic from a foal and know that he has a solid foundation. He'll make a good horse for us someday. We have no idea what these girls' personalities are like or what they've been through."

Rosie sighed. She knew her grandmother was right, but she still wished they could buy them.

They walked on but didn't find any ponies in the remaining pens. When they reached the end of the overhead walkway, they went down the stairs. Grandma glanced at her watch. "That worked out just right. By the time we make it back to the front of the auction house, the sale should be ready to start."

11

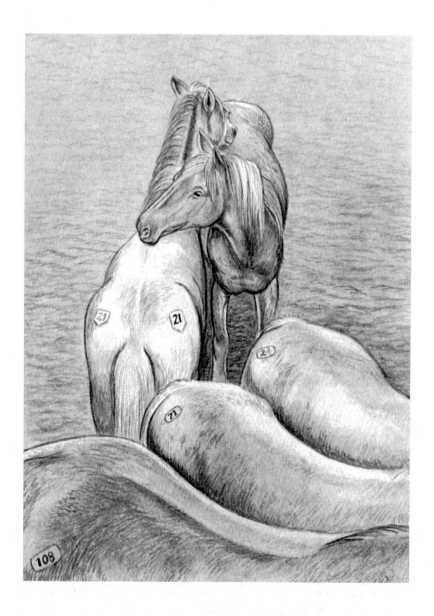

Grandma and the girls climbed the dark stairway at the front of the auction house and entered the sale area. The girls found seats in the top row while their grandmother registered as a buyer. Rosie

12

was surprised at how warm and stuffy it was inside the room. The sale pen below was small with a raised platform at the back for the auctioneer. Rosie figured when the auction started someone would lead a horse in through one of the doors on either side of the platform.

Grandma made it to her seat just as the sale began.

The door on the right opened. Rosie could see a man in the shadowy area behind it flicking a long buggy whip to drive the first horse into the arena. She gulped. They weren't hurting the horse, but this wasn't what she had expected. When the frightened animal entered the auction pen, he trotted around with his head high, facing the outside as if searching for a way to escape.

The auctioneer didn't waste any time trying to drive up the bids. There were only a couple people interested in this one, and he sold quickly for $300. The door on the left opened, and another man flicked at the horse with a whip until it ran out that side. The sale continued in the same manner, with horses coming in from the right, then rushed out on the left after the bidding ended. Rosie was surprised by how fast it all went.

She caught her breath when she saw a pale nose appear through the right-hand door.

Soon the two cremello mares rushed into the ring together. Rosie gave her grandmother a hopeful glance. Maybe she had changed her mind about buying them. Grandma shook her head and nodded toward two women sitting off to their right. The women wore matching blue shirts with "Shiloh Horse Rescue" printed on the back. Rosie was relieved when they purchased both of the mares.

It seemed like forever, but it was only twenty minutes before Rascal—or Jeremiah, or whatever his name was—pranced into the ring. Rosie grabbed Lauren and Carrie's hands and squeezed. The auctioneer started the bidding at $40.

Grandma held up the card with her number on it. Rosie smiled and pounded the girls' clenched hands on her knees until Carrie and Lauren shook free from her grasp.

13

For a moment, it appeared that no one else was going to bid, then one of the Shiloh Horse Rescue women said, "$50."

"Why are they bidding against us?" Rosie said in a not-very-quiet whisper.

Grandma bid again. "$75."

When the rescue woman looked their way, Rosie smiled and waved to her.

"Okay," the woman mouthed. She turned back around and didn't bid again.

No other buyers were interested in the small chestnut pony. Soon the auctioneer called out, "Sold for $75!"

Rosie was so eager to go welcome the newest addition to Sonrise Stable; she tripped over Carrie as she jumped up from the bench.

3

Rosie's Idea

D id you know there's an angel called Gabriel in here?" Billy looked up from his Bible. "Is that who little Gabe was named after?"

Rosie pulled out a chair beside Billy and sat down. "Where did you see that?"

"Right here." He pushed his open Bible across the table toward her and pointed to Luke 1:26.

Not that long ago, Billy had told her he didn't remember ever reading a book—not even in school. He was certainly reading a lot now.

Rosie found the passage he mentioned and read it silently. "Hmm. I knew an angel told Mary she would have the baby Jesus, but I forgot that his name was Gabriel. That's really cool."

Lauren walked into the meeting room of the activity barn. "What's really cool?"

"Gabriel was the name of the angel that appeared to Mary," Rosie said. "Like our little Gabe."

Lauren pointed to the clock on the wall. "Did you guys start without me? It's just now ten o'clock."

"No," Rosie said. "We're waiting for the Js to arrive."

Carrie patted the seat of the chair on the other side of her. "Here, sit beside me."

Jared, Jessie, and Jamie were the remaining three cousins who were part of the Bible study. After Jared had become a Christian that summer, he and Rosie had started the group. They met once a week in the activity barn. Now Billy had joined the study as well. Their group seemed small in the large room that was designed to hold a hundred or more children during their summer camps.

Billy picked up his Bible again. "I decided to read the whole New Testament. I'm in Luke now—reading about the first Christmas. I thought it was interesting when I saw the name Gabriel."

"Gabe should be here any day," Carrie said. "I can't believe how long it's taking."

Rosie nodded. "Every morning I wake up thinking it will be the day he comes, but then—"

"Hey, everyone!" Jared burst into the room with Jessie and Jamie right behind him. "Sorry we're late."

"We ran into Abigail at the barn," Jamie explained.

Jessie rolled her eyes. "And Jared preached an entire sermon to her."

"I did not," Jared laughed. "I invited her to the Bible study."

Rosie swallowed the lump that had suddenly formed in her throat, and her eyes shifted to the door. Apparently, Abigail hadn't accepted Jared's invitation. Thank goodness. It had been almost a month since the trail ride, but things were still tense between the two girls. It would be awkward to have her join their group.

"Is she going to come?" Lauren asked.

"Not this time," Jared said. "She had Raja saddled and was going out to ride."

Rosie sighed in relief, then glanced around to see if anyone had noticed. She should want Abigail to join them, but it was difficult for her to like the girl. More than difficult—it seemed impossible. She was honestly surprised Abigail's parents were still boarding Raja at Sonrise Stable. After the disastrous trail ride, she thought they would pack their horse up and move him to another farm.

Jessie sat down next to Rosie. "Patches and I are going to win the trail ride next year!"

"You don't even know if Mom will let us be in it," Jamie said.

"She will," Jessie insisted. "And I won't have to compete against Rosie and Abigail since they're banned from the ride!"

"Jessie, that's mean." Lauren glanced at Rosie.

"It's all right." Rosie waved her hand. She didn't like the endless rehashing of the events of the trail ride, but Jessie, in particular, couldn't seem to let it go.

After the competition, the 4-H leaders had met to listen to both Rosie's and Abigail's versions of what had happened during the ride. Although Rosie had finished the race first, she and Abigail were both disqualified for unsportsmanlike conduct and were not permitted to compete in next year's race. First place was awarded to Sarah Davis and her horse, Nugget.

"This was Abigail's last year as a junior," Billy said, "so you wouldn't compete against her anyway."

"If only I had a horse." Lauren frowned. "I'd love to be in the race."

"If you don't get one before next year, you could use Sassy," Billy offered. "She's an expert on those trails now."

"Thanks, Billy." Lauren smiled at him. "Maybe I'll have to do that."

Lauren and her parents had moved from Texas to join the rest of the family at Sonrise Stable. They had recently finished building a log cabin at the back of the property. Lisa and Robert had been so busy with that project; they hadn't had time to look for a horse. It was generous of Billy to offer Sassy. Rosie hadn't thought about letting

Lauren ride Scamper in the race. She wasn't allowed to compete, but what about Scamper. Was he banned too?

"Carrie, are you going to be in the race again?" Jamie asked.

"No." She shook her head. "I'll watch you two."

"Are you scared?" Jessie asked.

Rosie glared at her cousin. She couldn't believe how insensitive Jessie could be at times.

"No," Carrie said. "I'd rather just ride for fun. Competing makes me too nervous."

Rosie pulled at the threads surrounding a hole in the knee of her jeans. The day of the trail ride was one she wished she could forget... but probably never would. She'd never been so frightened in her life as when Carrie was lost on the trail.

Jessie crouched behind the table. "I want something exciting to happen when *I'm* in the trail ride," she leaped up and roared, "like a wild lion stalking us! Patches would protect me. She'd rear and strike the lion right on the head! That old lion would run away with his tail between his legs."

Jared pulled on his sister's arm. "Knock it off! That's not funny. A lion could easily kill a horse."

"Did you really see a lion?" Jamie asked Carrie.

Would the questions about the trail ride ever end? It had been a favorite topic of conversation the past few weeks. Every time they discussed it, Rosie felt slightly sick to her stomach.

Carrie shrugged. "I don't know. I thought I did, but I don't remember much after I got lost—until I was riding back with Billy on Sassy."

"Sassy the Super Mule was the hero." Billy grinned. "And she's also the star of the Christmas story."

Rosie had no idea what Billy meant, but she welcomed the diversion. "Oh? Sassy's in the Christmas story?"

20

Jessie leaned over and glanced at his Bible. "What are you reading? The NSV? The New Sassy Version?"

Billy turned his Bible over and looked at the cover. "Version? It says the Holy Bible. I didn't know there were different versions."

"Well," Rosie prodded him, "are you going to explain how your mule got into the Christmas story?"

"Mary rode a donkey to Bethlehem, didn't she? Donkey, mule—almost the same thing."

"Yeah, right." Rosie smiled. Billy knew there was a big difference between a donkey and a mule. Was he trying to spare her from all the talk about the trail ride?

"Actually, the Bible doesn't say Mary rode a donkey," Carrie pointed out.

"Oh yes it does!" Jessie opened her Bible.

"Yeah, I thought it did too," Jamie agreed with her sister.

"No, it doesn't," Lauren said.

Jared waved his hands. "Hold on, everyone. Let's pray first, and then we'll read the story to see exactly what it does say."

When Jared finished praying, he opened his Bible to the second chapter of Luke. "Lauren, would you read the first seven verses?"

And it came to pass in those days, that there went out a decree from Caesar Augustus that all the world should be taxed.

(And this taxing was first made when Cyrenius was governor of Syria.)

And all went to be taxed, every one into his own city.

And Joseph also went up from Galilee, out of the city of Nazareth, into Judaea, unto the city of David, which is called Bethlehem; (because he was of the house and lineage of David:)

To be taxed with Mary his espoused wife, being great with child.

And so it was, that, while they were there, the days were accomplished that she should be delivered.

And she brought forth her firstborn son, and wrapped him in swaddling clothes, and laid him in a manger; because there was no room for them in the inn.

"See." Billy pointed to a verse. "Mary and Joseph traveled from Nazareth to Bethlehem."

"Right." Carrie nodded. "But it doesn't say she rode a donkey."

Jessie pulled a sheet of paper out of her Bible and unfolded it. "How else would they get there? Ride a bus? Take a taxi?"

An image flashed into Rosie's mind of kind Joseph leading Mary on a gentle donkey, but she realized that picture was from Christmas stories or movies and not from the Bible. "Maybe they walked."

"How far is it from Nazareth to Bethlehem?" Jared flipped to the map section at the back of his Bible. "That might tell us if they could have walked there. I mean, she was about ready to have a baby. She couldn't have walked too far."

Jessie looked up from the picture she was drawing—a very round Mary on a spindly-legged donkey. "How would you know? You've never had a baby before."

"Like you have either." Jared took the paper Jessie was drawing on. "Oh wow! That poor donkey!"

"Give it back!" Jessie jumped up and grabbed the paper from him.

Carrie held up her Bible. "Listen to this study note. 'The journey from Nazareth to Bethlehem was seventy to ninety miles. As a carpenter, Joseph would have likely owned a donkey to carry wood. It's entirely plausible that Mary could have ridden a donkey; however, since the Bible doesn't mention it, we can't be certain.'"

Billy frowned. "I don't see how Mary could have walked ninety miles when she was 'great with child.'"

"I wouldn't want to take a bumpy donkey ride that far either if I was about to have a baby." Rosie swayed back and forth in her chair as if she were riding a donkey.

"A camel might be even worse," Carrie said. "I don't know for sure, since I've never ridden one, but anyway Joseph was too poor to own a camel."

"Oh, wow. I never thought about this before." Jared tapped a finger on his open Bible. "I always thought they arrived in Bethlehem the night Jesus was born, but it doesn't say that either."

Rosie read verse 6 again, "And so it was, that, while they were there, the days were accomplished that she should be delivered. You're right. It says, 'while they were there.'"

"Well, however and whenever they got there," Jared said, "there wasn't any place for them to stay."

"What do you mean?" Billy asked. "I was so focused on the donkey part I missed that."

"Verse 7." Jared read it aloud, "There was no room for them in the inn."

"What was wrong with those people?" Billy shook his head. "Didn't they know it was Jesus? Why didn't they *make* room for Him?"

"Of course they didn't know it was Jesus." Jessie was now working on a drawing of a manger with several sheep lying around it. "How could they know that? He hadn't even been born yet."

"That's why he was born in a barn," Jamie added.

"Technically," Carrie began, "it doesn't say that either."

Billy smiled. "You're full of technicalities today."

Carrie shrugged. "I'm not trying to be a pain. I just think our ideas about Christmas should match what's in the Bible. Luke says there wasn't any room in the inn and that the baby was placed in a manger."

Jessie raised an eyebrow and tilted her head to look at Carrie. "Where else would you have a manger—in your living room?"

"You're right," Carrie laughed. "It must have been a barn or stable."

"Like Sonrise Stable?" Billy said.

Rosie nodded. "I remember when Grandma read the Christmas story to me out in the barn. It made it seem so real."

"Real cold, you mean," Carrie said. "I wonder if it gets as cold in Bethlehem in the winter as it does in Ohio?"

Billy leaned back in his chair and stretched his long legs. "I never liked to read before, but I like reading the Bible. It's starting to make more sense to me."

That was one good result of the trail ride: Billy had been saved. Rosie smiled at him. "Grandma says learning the Bible is like putting a jigsaw puzzle together. Every time you learn something new, you fit another piece into the puzzle, and you can see the picture more clearly."

"I have a few pieces together," Billy said. "But there's one thing I don't understand."

"What's that?" Jared asked.

"Where does Santa Claus fit into all this?"

Rosie thought Billy was joking. "You won't find Santa in the Bible."

"Duh! I know that. But, really, I'm serious. How did we ever get from the story of baby Jesus, and maybe a donkey, to Santa and a herd of reindeer?"

The two stories were quite different. Reindeer pulling a sleigh full of toys for children through the air versus a shaggy donkey carrying a young woman who was soon to be the mother of God's Son over the rough countryside of Israel.

Jessie grinned. "I know what I want Santa to bring—"

Suddenly Rosie jumped up. "Oh! Oh! I'm getting an idea!"

Jessie jumped up too and backed quickly away from her. "Oh no! Are you contagious?"

Rosie ignored her cousin and paced back and forth across the room, patting the top of her head in rhythm with her steps. "Yes! It just might work!"

Everyone stared at her.

"Let's do it here!" Rosie said.

Carrie gave her a blank look. "Do what here?"

"Act out the Christmas story!"

"Sassy wants to be Rudolph," Billy joked.

"You know what I mean." Rosie punched him on the arm. "The real Christmas story—a live nativity scene!"

"That's a great idea!" Jared said. "We can decorate the farm like it was Bible times and invite tons of people to come see it."

Rosie nodded. "We'll each be one of the Bible characters."

"I'm going to be Mary!" Jessie shouted.

25

"I'll supervise," Billy said. "I'm terrible at acting. I was kicked out of the only play I was ever in—Mrs. Sherwood's class, second grade. I couldn't read then and kept stumbling over my lines. Whew! She was mean."

Rosie rolled her eyes at him. "You're making that up."

"It's the truth," Billy insisted. "Since I flunked acting, I won't be in it, but Sassy can be the donkey Mary rides." He gave a quick look at Carrie. "I mean, if we're going to use a donkey in the story."

"Little Gabe can be baby Jesus," Jamie suggested.

Rosie was glad to see everyone excited about her idea. Of course, they'd have to get their parents' approval, but she was certain they would love the idea too. Now she had to figure out a way to use Rascal and Charley in the live nativity.

4

Harness Training Begins

"Someone grab that pony!"

Rosie was cleaning harness in the barn aisle with Carrie. She jerked her head up to see a small chestnut pony running toward them, head high in the air, with Grandma chasing after him. "Look, Carrie!" she pointed and laughed. Rascal trotted rapidly, carefully placing his hooves to avoid stepping on the lead rope that trailed on the ground beside him.

Rosie didn't often see her grandmother run, although you couldn't really call what she was doing right then running—more like a super fast walk with a funny little hop or skip thrown in every once in a while. Rosie was enjoying the spectacle so much that she didn't think about trying to help.

"Stop, you little rascal!" Grandma caught up with him, but when she bent over to grab the end of the lead rope, he darted off sideways, and the rope flew out of her reach.

"Come on, Carrie!" Rosie dropped the harness and ran to help.

When Rascal saw the girls coming, he seemed to grin. Apparently, he considered this a great game—people tag! The pony skidded to a stop and whirled around to run the other direction, but

Grandma was right behind him. He escaped her grasp and pivoted to the left, but Carrie was there.

She grabbed the rope attached to his halter. "Got you! You little rascal!" The pony rubbed his head against Carrie's side and stamped a hoof, upset that the game had ended so soon.

Grandma wiped the sweat from her forehead with the back of her hand. "Whew! I need to keep a tighter hold on this guy the next time I get him out. I wasn't expecting him to take off like that."

In the short time he'd been at Sonrise Stable, Rascal had demonstrated several times how he had earned his name. Until the vet could examine him, they were keeping the pony in the round pen away from the other horses. Rascal was not at all happy with that arrangement.

To discover how he kept escaping, one day Rosie hid behind a tree and watched. Rascal wiggled the latch with his mouth until it raised enough for him to push the gate open. After that, she had started snapping a chain around the gate.

Rosie thought back to the Amish brothers who had previously owned Rascal. It seemed her grandmother's suspicions about their honesty had been right. The pony was proving to be much more a Rascal than a Jeremiah!

Grandma leaned against the barn wall and caught her breath. "How are you doing with the harness?"

"Let me tie him up first then we'll show you." Carrie tied Rascal to the hitching post, and then they all walked into the barn.

The two sets of harness Grandma had purchased at the sale were spread across the floor of the barn aisle. It was obvious the grimy, moldy tack had not been used in years. Some elbow grease and an entire jug of neatsfoot oil were transforming the stiff harness into soft, supple leather.

Tick, the Rottweiler, had to stay in the house while the girls worked. The dog had a craving for anything with neatsfoot oil on it. Rosie thought the oil smelled gross, but she understood how Tick felt. She was the same way with ketchup. It was hard to resist putting it on everything she ate.

Rosie picked up the long leather strap she was working on and held it out to her grandmother. "How's this?"

Grandma flexed the leather. "Much better. You girls are doing a great job. Leather will last a long time if it's taken care of."

Rosie stared at the pile in front of her. "This seems like a lot of harness for two small ponies. What do you need all these pieces for?"

"This one is called a trace. It's used to. . ." Grandma's voice trailed off, and she dropped the harness back on the ground. "You know, it would be easier to explain what each piece is for, if the harness was on one of the ponies. We might as well start right now getting our boys used to wearing it."

"Yay!" Rosie said.

The kids had explained to the adults their plan to act out the events of the first Christmas. Rosie hadn't been able to come up with a way to work the ponies into the story, so she and Carrie decided they would give children cart rides—driving them around to each of the scenes. It was already the end of September. That didn't leave much time to get the ponies ready.

Grandma pointed. "We'll need that piece right there. That's the saddle."

Rosie ran her fingers over the narrow, padded piece of harness. "Ouch! I'd hate to ride on this thing!"

Carrie and Grandma rolled their eyes at her attempt at humor.

"A couple pieces of harness have the same names as riding tack, but they obviously serve different purposes." Grandma pointed out another piece for Carrie to bring. "We don't need to use it all right now. Let's see how Rascal does with this much."

The girls carried the harness out front where Rascal was tied and stood at the pony's left side.

"We'll put this much of the harness on and walk him around so he gets used to the feel of it," Grandma said. "After you girls see how to do this with Rascal, you can do the same with Charley."

"Can't we work with them together?" Carrie asked.

"As soon as Rascal gets a clean bill of health from the vet, we will." Grandma nodded to Rosie. "Set the saddle on his back, behind his withers."

Rosie placed the saddle on Rascal's back with the straps hanging down on either side. "Like that?" The harness seemed a bit mysterious. She had ridden for years, but had never driven a pony.

Grandma slid the saddle back. "It sits further behind the withers than a riding saddle. That wider strap hanging down from it is the girth."

Rosie reached under the pony's tummy and pulled the girth strap up from the other side. "I know what this is." She buckled the girth so the saddle was held firmly in place. "What's the other strap beside it?"

"That's called the bellyband. Go ahead and fasten that one too. It doesn't need to be as tight as the girth."

"That's a funny name. What's it for?" Rosie buckled the strap behind the girth.

"See this part?" Grandma touched a leather loop halfway down the pony's side. "That's the tug. There's one on each side. The shafts of the cart slide through them."

"Oh. I get it," Rosie said. "They hold the cart in place."

"Partly. There's a little more to it than that, but we'll add the rest another day."

Carrie held up a long piece. "Where does this go?"

"That's the breastplate."

"Oh, I think I know." Carrie unbuckled a strap near the front of the breastplate and slipped it around Rascal's chest.

"That's it." Grandma nodded. "The top strap goes up over his neck and fastens here on the left side. Not surprisingly, it's called the neck strap."

Rosie watched Carrie fasten the buckle. Connected to each end of the breastplate were long leather straps, which, if extended to their full length, would be longer than Rascal. "The ends of those hook onto the cart?"

"Right. Those are the traces. We won't need those until we're ready for the cart." Grandma ran the long straps under the bellyband, then pulled them up and crisscrossed them over Rascal's back.

Was that all they were going to do? Lead Rascal and Charley around? Rosie was ready to start driving the ponies as soon as the carts were finished. Billy and Jared had sanded them down for painting and were working on new seats for each. The carts stood up on end beside the barn.

"When are we going to hook them to the carts?" Rosie couldn't wait to drive Rascal for the first time.

"Slow and steady," Grandma reminded her. "We'll take small steps. Remember how we trained Scamper?"

Rosie had suspected her grandmother would say something like that. They had begun working with Scamper when the orphaned foal was very young, leading him with lightweight things on his back. But Scamper's training had taken years. They only had a few months to get the ponies ready for the live nativity.

Grandma stepped back to check Rascal. "Everything looks good. Let's walk him around the driveway."

Rosie walked on the pony's left side and Carrie on his right. Grandma stood in the middle of the circular drive watching them. Rascal seemed a little nervous at first. He kept breaking into a trot and dancing around, but after a couple trips around the driveway, he became accustomed to the feel of the leather straps. Since he wasn't worried about the harness anymore, he entertained himself by trying to bite the end of the lead rope that dangled from Rosie's hand.

31

"You're a funny boy, Rascal." Rosie patted the pony. "I can't wait until Carrie and I can drive you and Charley."

Carrie pointed to a page in her Bible. "This study note says that the stable where Jesus was born might actually have been a cave."

The kids were continuing to investigate the Christmas story so they could make the nativity at Sonrise Stable as accurate as possible.

"Let me see." Rosie slid to the edge of her chair and read the note. Carrie hadn't been a Christian for that long, but she had already learned a lot about the Bible. Rosie realized she wasn't studying nearly as much as her sister was. It wasn't a contest, but she decided to start reading her Bible first thing every morning.

Carrie read the note aloud. "Despite the many nativity sets depicting the baby Jesus in a wooden stable, He may have been born in a cave."

"A cave? That's cool!" Jessie jumped out of her chair. "I know where we could make one!" She turned to Rosie. "You remember that big ravine beside the trail right before you get to Lauren's log cabin?"

Rosie nodded, but she didn't see what that had to do with the nativity.

"We could throw a stick of dynamite down there and blast out a big hole!" Jessie waved her arms up over her head and out to the sides. "That would make a sweet cave!"

Jared put both hands on his sister's shoulders and guided her back to her seat. "Sit down. No one's going to dynamite anything around here. Where do you get such crazy ideas?"

"There's more," Carrie continued. "Shepherds often used the caves that dotted the Judean countryside to protect their sheep from bad weather. It was also common for homes to have a cave-like stable below the main floor as a shelter for animals. The Lamb of God may have been born in such a structure."

"Yeah!" Jessie continued. "I think dynamite would definitely work."

Billy laughed. "How are we going to get people to your dynamite cave all the way at the back of our hundred acres?"

"Charley and Rascal will pull them in the carts."

Jamie frowned at her twin sister. "Only a few people could ride in each cart. That would take forever."

Jessie thought for a moment. "Oh! I have a better idea! Donkey rides! We can buy a whole herd of donkeys for people to ride from the barn to the cave—like they do at the Grand Canyon."

Rosie smiled. She was glad to see her younger cousin excited about the nativity, even if her idea was a bit far-fetched.

"That's a cool idea," Lauren agreed. "It would certainly make it realistic."

"I hate to rain on your parade," Billy said, "but your parents aren't going to buy a stable full of donkeys for a one-day event."

Jessie wasn't ready to give up that easily. "We could rent them."

"Yeah, right," Jared laughed. "Have you seen any Rent-a-Donkey places around here?"

Jessie crossed her arms and slumped back in her seat. "You guys don't like any of my ideas."

"It's a great idea, Jess. We just can't do it." Rosie pulled out a piece of paper. "Let's make a list of the animals and other things we'll need for the nativity."

"We can contact farms to see if we can borrow the animals that we don't have," Lauren suggested, "like sheep and goats."

"Don't forget the donkeys," Jessie mumbled.

"Will Gabe be the baby Jesus?" Jamie asked.

"That would be cute," Rosie said, "but he'll be about six months old by then."

"That's pretty big for a newborn!" Lauren said.

"I'm going to be Mary," Jessie insisted. "And I want Gabe to be baby Jesus!"

There was no way Gabe could be baby Jesus. He'd be able to crawl right out of the manger by then. Rosie's heart did a flip-flop whenever she thought about the little boy. Her parents expected him to arrive any day.

5

Gabe

ᴥ

Charley was delighted when Rascal finally joined him in the pasture. The first day they were together, they chased each other all around the field, then rolled in Charley's favorite dusty spot, and stood side by side dozing under an apple tree.

The girls walked to the pasture to catch the ponies for another training session. "I'm glad we can work with them together now." Rosie caught Rascal and snapped a lead to his halter. "Rascal needs a good example to follow."

Rosie and Carrie led the ponies to the center of the arena where their dad and grandmother waited. Grandma would help Carrie with Charley, and Eric and Rosie would work together with Rascal.

"Today we'll add the last part—the breeching and the crupper. They're connected together." Grandma held up the leather loop at the end. "This is the crupper. Their tail goes through that."

The breeching was a little confusing. Rosie held it up a couple of different ways. Her dad tried to help her figure it out, but he had less experience with horses than she did. Rosie was glad he was helping her though. Sometimes the rambunctious pony needed a strong hand to keep him under control. She knew more about horses, but her dad was much stronger, so they made a good team.

Rosie turned the breeching around so the crupper was at the top right.

Her grandmother nodded. "That's it. His tail goes through the crupper, and those wider straps at the bottom go around his hindquarters. The strap at the top that runs down the middle of his back is called the back strap. That connects the whole thing to the saddle."

"Oh. I see." Rosie unbuckled the crupper and positioned it around Rascal's tail. She jumped sideways when Rascal stomped his hind leg as if he was about to kick. "Easy, boy. This won't hurt you."

She gradually moved the crupper up until it was under the base of Rascal's tail, then fastened the buckle around it. The pony hopped forward like a giant bunny rabbit, but Eric held on to him. When Rascal stood still again, Rosie pulled the back strap forward and snapped it to the saddle. "There! It's on."

Grandma and Carrie were having a much easier time with Charley. He didn't mind the crupper at all and stood calmly as Carrie finished harnessing him.

"I better lead Rascal first," Eric said, "until he gets used to walking with his new gear on."

Gear? Rosie had never heard harness called that before. She smiled at her dad's terminology, then hurried out of Rascal's way. The pony had jumped again as if he thought he could leap out of the harness. Rosie was glad her dad was leading him. Even though he was small, Rascal was strong and could easily get away from her.

Rosie watched her dad try to convince the pony to walk calmly. "Why is Rascal acting so crazy?"

"The crupper feels weird to them," Grandma said. "It's the hardest part of the harness for them to get used to."

It took several trips around the arena, but Rascal finally settled down. Next, the girls attached long reins to the ponies' driving bridles and ran the reins through metal rings called turrets on the saddle to keep them from dragging on the ground.

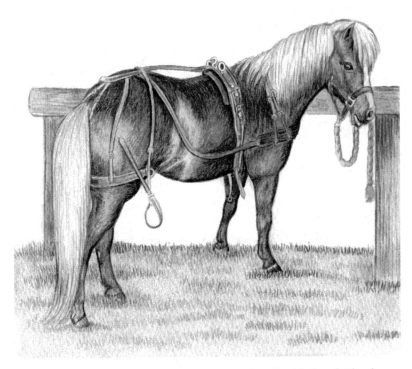

The girls held the ends of the reins and walked behind Charley and Rascal, far enough back to avoid being kicked. Ground driving would teach the ponies to respond to the reins and voice commands before they were hooked to a cart.

"Gee!" Rosie called out.

Carrie started to turn Charley to the left.

"No. No. Right, right."

"Do we have to use *gee* and *haw*? Can't we say right and left?" Carrie frowned. "It's too confusing. I can't remember whether *gee* means right and *haw* means left or the other way around."

"I don't know who started using those words." Rosie turned Rascal to the right. "Grandma says they're easier for the horses to understand. And, if the ponies hear a person say 'left' or 'right'

37

in conversation, they might think someone was giving them commands. Other people aren't likely to say 'gee' and 'haw.'"

Rosie steered Rascal to a practice trail bridge in the arena. "Dad, Grandma. Watch this!" The pony stopped in front of it, lowered his head, and sniffed.

"Get up." She clucked to him. "Come on, boy. You can do it."

Rascal placed one small hoof on the wooden bridge, then another. His hooves made a clopping sound as he crossed over it. Rosie stepped down off the other side.

"Impressive! He's a quick learner," Grandma said.

"And he has a good trainer," her dad added.

Rosie beamed. They were getting closer to the day she'd be able to drive Rascal.

Grandma had been right about the carts. Billy and Jared had worked on them until they looked almost like new. They had painted them black, and both now had a padded leather seat.

Rosie couldn't wait until Charley and Rascal would pull the carts, but for now, the kids were having fun pulling each other around the barnyard in them.

"Where, Mom?"

"Right there." Kristy pointed to the back corner of the kitchen by the table.

Rosie carried the broom and dustpan and swept up a few pieces of dirt from the floor.

"Over here please, Carrie." Kristy put her finger on a smudgy area of the window in the back door. "See that spot?"

"Mom, why do we have to clean all this? Gabe's three months old. He can't even crawl yet."

Kristy smiled and sat down at the table. "I'm sorry. I guess I *am* going a little overboard. I clean when I'm nervous."

Rosie sat on her mother's lap.

"Oomph!" Kristy wrapped her arms around the twelve-year-old and squeezed. "You're getting so big. It seems like only yesterday you were Gabe's size. Are you excited about having a baby brother?"

"Sometimes I don't think I can wait another second! Oops!" Rosie jumped up and grabbed the broom. "I see another dust bunny."

Carrie tossed a dirty paper towel into the trash. "What time is Gabe coming?"

Kristy glanced at the clock on the stove. "He should be here any minute."

Rosie felt her stomach turn. They'd been waiting so long for her little brother to arrive. She'd seen him a few times on visits to the county office and couldn't wait to hold him again.

"Why don't you girls see if Grandma needs help?" Kristy nodded toward the stairway. "We've cleaned everything we can in here."

The girls raced upstairs to their grandmother's room and found her at her sewing machine with Tick stretched out on the floor by her feet. Her bob-tailed calico cat, June Bug, was asleep on the window sill.

Lauren stood in the middle of the room on a chair, arms out to her sides, with a blue sheet draped over her.

"All right. That's all I needed. Take it off, and let me work on that piece," Grandma said.

"What are you supposed to be?" Rosie laughed at Lauren.

"What do you think?" Lauren pulled the sheet off.

Rosie plopped onto the bed. "Superman?"

"Don't you know a shepherdess when you see one?" Lauren said.

"Oh, right!" Rosie rolled over and noticed a pile of costumes on the floor beside her grandmother. "I didn't realize an army of shepherds came to the stable to see the baby Jesus."

Grandma paused the machine to look at the stack. "Oh, dear! You're right. I guess we won't need quite that many."

Rosie laughed. Her mom cleaned when she was nervous, and her grandmother sewed.

Carrie wandered over to the window.

"Do you see anyone yet?" Grandma asked.

She shook her head. "I don't know what kind of car they have, but I don't see anyone at all."

Grandma picked up a costume and examined it. "I guess I can turn this into an outfit for the innkeeper."

"Was there an innkeeper in the Christmas story?" Carrie asked.

"Oh no," Lauren said. "Here we go again."

"Sorry." Carrie smiled. "Just wondering."

"We can check into that at our next Bible study," Rosie suggested.

"How many animals have you located for the nativity?" Grandma turned her sewing machine off and shifted in her chair to face the girls.

"Hold on. Let me get my notebook." Rosie ran to her room and returned with a spiral-bound tablet she'd been keeping notes in. "Let's see. So far, we have six sheep and three goats. And Aunt Julie knows someone who will loan us a donkey named Gus. In fact, her friend said we could keep him if we wanted to."

"We have plenty of animals here already without adding a donkey to the menagerie," Grandma said. "We don't need the expense of feeding an animal we'd only use once a year."

"Will Billy be upset that we're using a real donkey instead of Sassy?" Carrie asked.

"Sassy's too big," Lauren said, "especially if Jessie is Mary."

"Do we have to let her be Mary?" Rosie knew Jessie had her heart set on playing that part, but she was too small to make it seem realistic.

"We'll determine who's taking each role soon," Grandma said. "I'm sure Billy and Jessie will both be fine with whatever we decide."

Rosie wasn't so sure about that. Billy would be all right, of course, but Jessie had her heart set on playing the part of Mary.

"Is Gabe too big to be baby Jesus?" Lauren asked.

"Yes," Grandma laughed. "Can you picture Jessie holding a fifteen-pound newborn on her lap?"

"Jessie's too small," Rosie said, "and Gabe's too—"

"They're here!" Carrie jumped up and down and pointed out the window.

Rosie ran to her side and saw a small red car making its way up the driveway. She leaned back against the wall. "No. That's Mrs. Miller."

Carrie looked puzzled. "Who?"

"Abigail's mom," Rosie replied.

"Oh, yeah. Sorry. I forgot about her."

When Abigail stepped out of the car, Rosie frowned. For the past month, she'd done her best to avoid the girl as much as possible. Seeing Abigail always reminded her of the bad experience at the trail ride. But this time, the sight of her prompted a sudden, crazy thought—what if Abigail gave Raja to Lauren for Christmas!

The girl still rode him, but not as much as she used to. Lauren needed a horse, and she would take great care of him. The more Rosie thought about it, the more excited she became. Plans flew around in her head. First, they'd move Raja to the stall next to Scamper and Zach—

RINGGG! RINGGG!

The sound of the phone downstairs jolted Rosie from her thoughts. All the adults in the family had cell phones, but occasionally people still called on the home phone. She glanced at Carrie and Lauren. "I wonder if that's about Gabe." She bolted for the door, followed by the other two. Tick, awakened by the noise, almost tripped the girls as she raced down the stairs after them. The dog had no way of knowing what the excitement was all about, but it didn't take much to get her wound up.

When they reached the bottom of the stairs, Tick barked and jumped up on Rosie. "No, girl. Down!" She took a deep breath to calm herself, and then walked into the living room. Her mother was talking on the phone.

"What?" Kristy walked across the room, looking down at the floor. She didn't look happy.

Rosie watched and listened, trying to determine whether she was talking to the foster agency or not.

"What do you mean?" Kristy said.

"Who is it, Mom?" Rosie whispered.

Kristy shook her head and waved her hand to hush her. "But I thought everything was settled?"

The expression on her mother's face alarmed Rosie. When Grandma arrived in the living room, Rosie leaned against her.

"Thanks for letting me know." Kristy slowly set the phone down.

Rosie could see tears in her eyes. "What is it, Mom? What's wrong?"

"He's not coming."

"What?" Rosie said. "You mean Gabe?"

Kristy nodded.

"He's not coming today?" Carrie frowned.

"When is he coming?" Lauren asked. "Tomorrow?"

When Rosie saw her grandmother wrap her arms around Kristy, she knew Gabe would not be coming tomorrow—or any day. "What happened?" She choked the words out.

"The court made a last-minute decision to send Gabe back to his mother." Kristy wiped her eyes and made a strange expression that Rosie guessed was supposed to be a smile.

"His mother?" Rosie didn't understand exactly how these things worked. Why had they changed their minds? She and Carrie had helped their mom paint one of the small rooms upstairs for the little boy. They had a crib with a Noah's ark comforter and everything. This was supposed to be his home now.

Kristy pulled a few tissues out of the box on the coffee table and blew her nose. She gave the girls each a hug. "Would you three do me a favor? Run out to the barn and check on Rascal to make sure he didn't get out again."

Rosie wiped tears from her eyes. "Okay, Mom." She knew the request meant that her mom wanted to talk to Grandma alone. Once Rascal had gone out with Charley, they hadn't had any more problems with him escaping.

Tick rubbed against Rosie's right side. The dog looked up at her and whined. She patted Tick's head. "Yes. You can go with us."

The three girls started toward the door. Rosie glanced back and saw her mom crying on Grandma's shoulder.

Gabe wasn't coming. It felt as if a small hole had been poked into her heart. She wouldn't be a big sister after all.

6

Operation Christmas Spirit

Rosie looked around the table at the others gathered for the weekly Bible study. Everyone was quiet. It had been nearly a week since they learned Gabe would not be joining their family. She still felt sad—like a balloon with the air leaking out of it.

Jared broke the silence. "How are the costumes coming?"

"Good," Lauren said. "Grandma's ready for an army of shepherds."

"Speaking of shepherds..." Rosie flipped her Bible open. "That's what's up next in Luke."

Billy leaned over to see where she was.

"Luke 2:8—16," Rosie informed them. When they all had located the passage, she read aloud.

And there were in the same country shepherds abiding in the field, keeping watch over their flock by night.

And, lo, the angel of the Lord came upon them, and the glory of the Lord shone round about them: and they were sore afraid.

And the angel said unto them, Fear not: for, behold, I bring you good tidings of great joy, which shall be to all people.

For unto you is born this day in the city of David a Saviour, which is Christ the Lord.

And this shall be a sign unto you; Ye shall find the babe wrapped in swaddling clothes, lying in a manger.

And suddenly there was with the angel a multitude of the heavenly host praising God, and saying,

Glory to God in the highest, and on earth peace, good will toward men.

And it came to pass, as the angels were gone away from them into heaven, the shepherds said one to another, Let us now go even unto Bethlehem, and see this thing which is come to pass, which the Lord hath made known unto us.

And they came with haste, and found Mary, and Joseph, and the babe lying in a manger.

Rosie set her Bible on the table. "I don't know much about sheep or shepherds. That's one animal we've never had at Sonrise Stable."

"I know one thing," Billy said. "Sheep have to be the dumbest animals in the world."

"Dumber than your mule?" Since Billy teased her so much, Rosie couldn't resist giving some of it back.

Billy nodded. "My dad raised sheep when I was a kid. Sassy is Einstein compared to the sheep we had. I'll never forget one old ewe. When I was little, about every time I took a bucket of grain out to feed them, she would charge at me and knock me flat on my back."

Jared tipped back in his chair. "Why'd she do that?"

"The grain spilled all over the ground; then she'd hurry and try to gobble it up before the other sheep arrived."

Lauren laughed. "Sounds to me like she was pretty smart."

Billy scratched his head. "Yeah. Smart in a stupid sort of way. That's how I first became interested in running. I had to get fast enough to outrun that crazy sheep."

Jessie tapped her pencil on the table. "Who went to the stable first—the shepherds or the kings?"

"The three wise men, you mean?" Billy asked.

Jessie nodded. "I think the kings should have been there first—"

"No," Carrie interrupted. "The kings didn't go to the stable."

"You mean the wise men weren't there?" Billy looked confused.

"Whoa," Jared said. "Let's save that story for next—"

"Can I have a piece of paper?" Jessie blurted.

Lauren tore a page out of her notebook and slid it over to Jessie.

"Back to the shepherds," Jared said. "What if you had been one of the shepherds that night?"

"I would have been scared," Lauren said. "But I bet it was exciting being in that field when an angel appeared out of nowhere."

Jessie leaped out of her chair and yelled loudly, "Shazam!"

Rosie jumped and stared at her cousin. With Jessie around, you never knew what was going to happen next.

Jessie spun around and continued in a loud voice, "Out of the black night with horrible vengeance, the Mighty Marvo!"

Rosie smiled. Jessie's dramatic rendition of the line from the book *The Best Christmas Pageant Ever* certainly captured the startling nature of the angel's appearance.

Jared smiled and guided his younger sister back to her seat.

"Was that Gabriel too?" Jamie asked. "That angel?"

Hearing that name made Rosie think of little Gabe again. She hoped his mom was taking good care of him. She hadn't asked too many questions about what had happened. Her mom was still upset about the way things had turned out.

"The Bible doesn't give any name for that angel," Carrie said.

"Wouldn't the shepherds be cold out in the fields on December 24?" Jamie asked.

Jessie stopped writing for a moment. "If they lived in Ohio, they'd have frostbite."

"No one knows for sure when Jesus was born," Jared said. "It might not have been in December."

Rosie leaned over to see what Jessie was writing. Her cousin slapped her hand down over the sheet of paper to hide it. That made Rosie more determined to see it. "What are you doing?"

"Nothing," Jessie snapped.

Jared quietly stepped up on the other side and swiped the paper from under his sister's hand. He held it up and read, "Riding boots, Qwirkle game, new bike, art set…"

"What is this?" He dropped the paper back onto the table. "Your Christmas list? It's still October!"

Jessie folded the paper and crammed it into her pocket. "Leave me alone!"

"Seriously?" Jared frowned. "We're studying the birth of Jesus, and all you can think about is what you want people to get you for Christmas?"

Jessie turned her back to her brother.

"Nobody ever gets me anything for Christmas." Billy slouched back in his chair.

Was Billy kidding? As Rosie studied him more carefully, she wondered. He didn't have the usual grin that indicated he was joking. Did he really not get anything for Christmas?

"I can't believe you're making a list," Jared muttered. "And in the middle of our Bible study. Presents aren't what Christmas is supposed to be about."

Jessie whirled around to face him. "Everybody gets presents for Christmas—even you!"

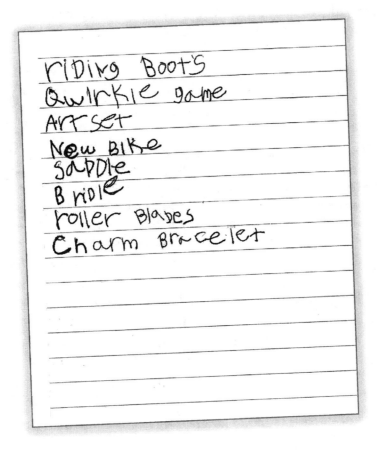

riding Boots
Qwirkle game
Art set
New Bike
Saddle
Bridle
roller Blades
Charm Bracelet

Jared sat back down at the table and stared at his sister for a moment. "Maybe we shouldn't."

"What?" The pencil fell out of Jessie's hand. "Are you kidding me?"

"That would be interesting." Carrie nodded slowly, apparently turning the thought over. "What if none of us received gifts this year?"

Rosie's mouth dropped open. She wasn't sure about this. It was fun to receive presents. What would they do on Christmas Day if they didn't exchange gifts? Every Christmas morning the family gathered and unwrapped their gifts. Then the cousins played together until it was time for dinner. Rosie couldn't believe Carrie didn't want any presents.

"What's wrong with getting gifts?" Jamie asked.

"It makes you keep thinking about the wrong things," Jared said. "Instead of focusing on Jesus, you think about what you're going to get."

As much as she hated to admit it, Rosie knew Jared was right. Last year her heart had been set on a new trail saddle for Scamper. A few days before Christmas, a large box appeared under the tree. Rosie was certain it was the saddle. She daydreamed about what it would feel like to ride Scamper with it. But as it turned out, the present hadn't even been for her. Her heart had been so set on getting the saddle; she was a little disappointed with the gifts that she did receive.

"Since Christmas is when we celebrate Jesus' birthday, why don't we give *Him* a gift?" Lauren suggested.

"We can't do that since He's in heaven, so we better give gifts to each other instead. I think Jesus wants us to do that," Jessie stated matter-of-factly as if that settled the matter.

"Nice try," Jared said. "Tell us where you found that in the Bible."

Jessie shrugged. "The Bible doesn't tell us *every single thing* we're supposed to do!"

"'Inasmuch as you did it to one of the least of these My brethren, you did it to Me.'" Lauren quoted Matthew 25:40. NKJV

"What do you mean?" Rosie asked.

"I think it means that if we give a gift to someone else, it's as close as we can come to giving a gift to Jesus," Lauren said.

"I'm confused," Jessie said. "We *are* getting gifts after all?"

"No, not *getting—giving*," Jared said. "We'll give gifts to other people."

"Like who?" Rosie still wasn't sold on the idea.

"Who's someone we could surprise with a gift?" Carrie asked. "Why don't we each come up with a name?"

"I don't have enough money to get anyone a gift," Jamie said.

"Let's say all the gifts have to cost little or nothing," Carrie said. "None of us have much money, so we could make things too."

Lauren agreed. "Christmas shouldn't be about money."

She didn't want to sound as selfish as Jessie, so Rosie grudgingly accepted the idea. She pointed to each of them and counted. "There are seven of us, so we'll need seven people. Start giving me names. I'll write them on pieces of paper, and then we'll each pick one."

"Kids or adults?" Lauren asked.

Jared shrugged. "It could be either."

"What about Mom?" Carrie suggested. "She's been really sad since Gabe didn't come to live with us. A gift might cheer her up."

Rosie pulled a sheet of paper out of her notebook and tore it into seven pieces. She wrote "Mom" on one of them. "Oops! I guess she's not everyone's mom." She crossed that out and wrote "Kristy."

"We should add Grandma," Jamie said. "She's always doing things for other people."

Rosie wrote that down next.

"This shouldn't just be about us," Jared said. "How about someone outside the family?"

"Annabelle!" Lauren said.

"How would we get a present to her?" Jamie asked. "We don't know where she lives."

Annabelle was a great suggestion. The rambunctious young girl had kept Rosie on her toes that first week of summer camp. "I bet Grandma saved all the camp registrations. We'll be able to get her address from that. Annabelle makes three names. We need four more."

"Abigail Miller," Jared said.

Rosie stared a moment at the blank piece of paper in her hand before she started writing. She was fine with it as long as someone else drew Abigail's name.

"We could add Mrs. Wilson," Jamie said.

"Who's Mrs. Wilson?" Lauren asked.

"Our neighbor," Jared explained. "Her husband died a few years ago. She's older and lives alone now."

As Rosie was writing down that name, she had an idea and motioned for Jared to come closer. She whispered to him, "I think we should put Billy in the drawing."

"Good idea," Jared whispered back. "But what if he picks his own name?"

She already had that worked out. "You ask him to pick first. I'll keep his name out, then after he picks, I'll slip it in with the others."

Jared smiled and nodded.

Jessie sat up in her seat. "What are you two whispering about? You're not supposed to have secrets in a Bible study!"

Rosie smiled at her. "We have one secret entry—a mystery person!" She wrote down Billy's name, folded the slip of paper, and waved it around in the air. She wanted to pick his name and knew exactly what she would make—a saddle blanket with "Sassy the Super Mule" stitched on it.

Rosie sighed when she noticed Jessie smiling broadly. She must think she's the mystery person.

"One more," Carrie said. "Anyone have a suggestion?"

"How about my dad?" Billy said. "Dad and I never used to do much for Christmas. He'll probably spend the day at home alone."

Not long after Billy came to work at Sonrise Stable, Rosie had learned that his mother died soon after Billy was born. Rosie had felt sad for Billy, but she hadn't thought about how lonely his dad must have been all those years. "That's a good idea! Should I write Mr. King?"

"His name is Daniel," Billy said.

Rosie wrote "Daniel King" on the last paper. She pressed her thumb against her palm in order to hold onto the one with Billy's name on it, then used both hands to shuffle the other pieces around.

"We'll each pick a name, and that will be the person you'll get or make a gift for." Jared stood and spun around in a circle, then he stopped with his finger pointing at Billy. "You first."

Billy picked up one of the pieces of paper, unfolded it, and started to speak, "I have—"

"No!" Jared waved his hands, stopping Billy before he could say the name. He held his index finger up to his mouth. "The name you pick has to be kept secret. No one is allowed to reveal who they have until Christmas Day."

Rosie scrambled the names again, this time dropping Billy's paper in with the rest. She shoved the pile of papers toward Lauren, who picked a name and pushed them on to the next person.

"The first time we meet after Christmas," Jared said, "we'll each tell what it was like: how we got the idea for the gift and how it felt to give it to our person."

Finally, it was Rosie's turn. She was beginning to feel excited about this idea. It would be fun to surprise someone with a gift. There was only one paper left on the table. She picked it up and slowly unfolded it—*Abigail?* How was that possible? She tried to smile so no one would see the disappointment on her face. She crumpled the paper and stuffed it into her pocket.

"What do you think of this, guys?" Lauren held up a piece of paper on which she had written, "Operation Christmas Spirit."

"I love it!" Carrie said.

Lauren had arranged the words in a decorative way with a sprig of holly at the bottom. Rosie had no idea her cousin was so artistic. She couldn't help feeling a little discouraged. She was supposed to be the artist in the family.

OPERATION CHRISTMAS SPIRIT

"That's perfect. Operation Christmas Spirit," Jared said. "We're all on a top-secret mission to capture the true spirit of Christmas."

"No gifts for us this year," Carrie added.

"Everyone agreed?" Lauren asked.

They all nodded...except Jessie.

"Come on, Jess," Jared said. "Aren't you going to join us?"

Jessie paused, then mumbled, "I guess so."

Rosie understood. Operation Christmas Spirit would have been fun if she had picked any of the other names. She didn't have a single idea of anything to give Abigail. Why did she have to draw that girl's name?

"You two have done such good work with these ponies." Eric walked toward the girls carrying some long, white, plastic pipes. He leaned them up against the arena fence where the girls were preparing to ground drive the ponies again.

"Hi, Dad." Rosie patted Rascal's neck. "He's a fast learner. Are we ready for the cart today?"

"Not yet, but we are ready for the next step." Eric pointed to the poles leaning against the fence.

"What are those?" Carrie asked.

"Practice shafts. When your grandmother explained how we needed to introduce things gradually with their training, especially with this guy," Eric pointed to Rascal, "I got the idea to make these training shafts from PVC pipes."

"They're perfect." Grandma ran a hand over the makeshift shaft. "This way Rascal and Charley can get used to how the shafts of a real cart feel."

"Why can't we use the real carts now?" Rosie asked.

"Some horses and ponies are frightened by a cart behind them," Grandma explained. "Carts make funny noises, and when you turn, the shafts press against their sides."

"They can't see the cart behind them either, right?" Carrie took Charley's halter off and started to bridle him.

"Right," Grandma agreed. "The ponies' bridles have what are called blinders that block their vision to the sides. That keeps them focused on their job—so they're not distracted by the things around them."

"Maybe I should use blinders so I can focus on my schoolwork," Rosie said.

"You might be on to something," Eric laughed. "You should suggest that to your mother."

Grandma picked up one of the shafts. "We'll use these for a while, and then we'll add some sound effects and heavier things for them to drag around. After that, they'll be ready for the carts."

Rosie nodded. It all made sense, but she was still impatient to begin driving.

Eric held Rascal by the bridle, while Grandma let him sniff the U-shaped shaft. Next, she rubbed the shaft along the pony's right side; then switched over and did the same on the opposite side.

Grandma stepped to the left of Rascal's hindquarters. "Rosie, go to the other side. Slide the end of the shaft through the tugs, those loops in the bellyband. Once you have the shaft in, wrap that strap from the breeching around the ring on the shaft. That's called the holdback strap. It keeps the shaft from moving too far forward and bumping him from behind."

When Rosie had everything connected, she stepped back and looked at Rascal. The pony stood quietly with the white plastic shafts along each side. Another pipe connected them at the back, behind his hindquarters, forming a U shape.

"Try walking him," Grandma said. "Once Rascal's going okay, we'll do the same with Charley."

Rosie gathered the long reins and positioned herself behind the pony. When she was ready, Eric let go of his head.

Rosie clucked and said, "Walk."

Grandma walked alongside Rascal. When they reached the end of the arena, she asked Rosie to turn the pony. "Be ready. When he turns sharply, the shafts pressing on his side may spook him."

"Haw." Rosie asked for a left turn. As Rascal turned, the shaft bumped his side. He looked back to see what was going on, but otherwise didn't seem bothered by it.

"Whew!" Rosie let out a breath. Maybe Rascal was beginning to trust them. She walked the pony around, waiting for Carrie and Charley to join them.

Rosie spotted Abigail coming from the barn toward the arena leading Raja. The girl glanced their way, then mounted her horse, and turned in the opposite direction, toward the woods. It seemed Abigail didn't want to be around her any more than she wanted to be around Abigail. Why had she picked that girl's name for Operation Christmas Spirit?

7

The Metallic Monster

No gifts? Not even from your mom and me?" Eric held
Rascal while Rosie harnessed him.

"None at all? Whose idea was that?" Grandma helped Carrie get
Charley's tail through the crupper.

The girls looked at each other, then nodded.

"We all agreed." Rosie fastened the last buckle on the harness.
"We're calling it Operation Christmas Spirit. We want to focus on
Christ's birth instead of gifts."

Rosie didn't reveal the rest of the operation—the gifts they
planned to give. She didn't want to ruin their surprise.

"What an interesting idea," Grandma said. "You kids are
challenging me. First the live nativity, now this. We adults could have
a no-gift Christmas too."

"Suits me." Eric grinned. "It will save money, and it's not like any
of us need anything."

Their idea had obviously surprised her dad and grandmother.
It would be fun to see Grandma receive a gift on Christmas, when
she wasn't expecting anything. Rosie hoped whoever had drawn her

name would make it something special. She wished once again that she had picked any name other than Abigail's!

Eric walked over and picked up something that was hanging over the arena fence.

"What's that, Dad?" Rosie asked.

With a grin, Eric dangled a thin rope with a dozen empty cans attached to it. When he moved his hand up and down, the cans clanked against each other.

Rosie stared at the contraption with its string of pop, baked beans, and vegetable cans. Her dad was really getting into his new role as a horse trainer. She had no idea what he planned to do with his latest creation. A vision of Rascal drinking a can of orange soda came to mind and made her smile. The cans must have been left from summer camp. Her mom only let them have pop on special occasions. "We're giving them pop so they'll have enough energy to pull the carts?"

"Very funny." Eric held out one string of cans to Rosie. "Here's one for you."

He handed the other set to Carrie. "And one for you. Tie those onto the back bar of the shafts. When the ponies move, the cans will drag along the ground and make a racket."

"I get it now." Rosie took the rope and tied it around the shaft that ran behind Rascal's hindquarters.

"They need to get used to noises behind them," Grandma explained. "Once they're comfortable with that, we'll attach something heavier so they get the feel of pulling weight too."

"Then can we hook up the carts?" Rosie asked.

"We'll do this for a few more days," Grandma said, "and then they should be ready for the carts."

"Yay!" Rosie couldn't wait for the first drive with Rascal. She adjusted the reins and clucked for the pony to walk. The cans clanked together as he stepped forward.

Rascal's ears flicked back, focusing like radar on the strange noise. He apparently thought a metallic monster was after him, because he jumped and tried to twist sideways. The pony ran several steps with Rosie flying along behind him, clinging tightly to the reins.

Eric raced after them and grabbed Rascal's bridle. "Whew! Sorry, Rosie. I should have led him first to make sure he wasn't afraid of the cans before turning him over to you. Grandma was right about taking all these baby steps before we add the cart." He turned the pony around, and they started back.

Rosie was glad her dad was there to take over. She walked alongside Rascal. "There's nothing to be afraid of, boy. You have to start trusting us."

They waited while Grandma and Carrie finished getting Charley ready.

"When Kristy was about your age," Grandma paused to fasten a buckle on the harness, "we tried to train her pony, Ebony, to pull a cart."

Her grandmother was about to launch into one of her stories. Rosie hadn't heard this one before, but the words "tried to train" made her think the story wasn't going to have a happy ending.

"Ebony had been driving beautifully for several weeks," Grandma continued. "One afternoon, I was ready to step into the cart for another drive when she spooked at something. Before I realized what was happening, she jerked the reins out of my hands and ran frantically in circles around the backyard. I watched helplessly as the frightened pony nearly crashed into the fence. Finally, the cart tipped over, the harness broke, and she was freed from it. When I caught her, Ebony was trembling and drenched in sweat."

Rosie's eyes widened. Training a pony to drive hadn't seemed like it would be that difficult. No wonder Grandma had been going slowly with the ponies' training. "Do you think Rascal or Charley would do that?"

"I don't believe Charley ever would, but I'm not so sure about Rascal," Grandma said. "We'll have to be extra careful with him."

"Did you keep driving her?" Rosie had never heard her mom talk about driving Ebony.

"No. Ebony smashed up the cart and ripped the harness in several places. She wasn't hurt, but she was scared so badly that I never drove her again. She was always a great pony under saddle, though."

Rosie patted Rascal. "It's okay, buddy. They're just cans. Trust me; cans won't hurt you."

"What if we walk them side by side?" Carrie suggested. "Charley isn't afraid of anything. Maybe Rascal will feel braver walking next to him."

Grandma nodded. "Good idea."

The girls set off together with Grandma walking at Charley's head and Eric at Rascal's. Charley plodded along, not bothered at all by the cans rattling behind him. Rascal seemed to gain confidence as he walked by his friend Charley's side. After a few laps around the arena, they stopped at the gate.

Rosie smiled. "He seems to be getting it."

"He's doing fine," Grandma agreed. "Let's stop for now. Remember, you should always end on a positive note. We'll work with them again tomorrow."

"You need to be a good boy, Rascal. We only have two months to get you ready to give cart rides at the nativity." Rosie untied the string of cans from the shaft and set them on the ground.

As the girls led the ponies into the barn, they met Abigail on her way out with Raja.

Rosie's mind flashed back to the Operation Christmas Spirit drawing, when she had unfolded the paper with the girl's name on it. She decided to make more of an effort to get along with her.

Rosie smiled. "Hi, Abigail."

"Hey." The girl didn't return the smile. "What are you doing with the twin midgets?"

How dare Abigail call their ponies midgets? Rosie's throat tightened and her temperature rose a few degrees, but she took a deep breath and forced herself to remain pleasant. "We were working on their harness training. How's Raja?"

Abigail tossed her head, then mounted the horse and rode off without replying.

"Don't listen to her, little buddy." Rosie sighed and rubbed Rascal's forehead. "You're not a midget; you just have short legs."

Charley started to turn and follow Raja, but Carrie pulled him back. "Why are you being so nice to Abigail all of a sudden?"

"I don't know. Maybe I'm getting the Christmas spirit." Rosie wished she could tell her sister about picking Abigail's name. Carrie could help her come up with gift ideas. But they had all promised to keep the names a secret. She'd have to be careful not to give it away.

After they groomed the ponies and turned them out in the pasture, Rosie and Carrie joined the others, who were gathered in the activity barn for their weekly Bible study.

"Operation Christmas Spirit is putting me in a bad mood." Jessie slouched back in her chair. "How in the world am I supposed to get someone I barely know a gift, especially when I don't have any money?"

Hmm, barely know. That narrowed down the possibilities for which name Jessie had. Even though she tried not to, Rosie found herself guessing whose name each of the others had.

"Shh." Jared waved at his sister. "You're not supposed to let anyone know who you have."

"I didn't say who I had!" Jessie insisted. "Can't I get someone to help me?"

65

"No," Rosie said. "Come on, Jess; keep trying. You'll come up with something. I don't have any ideas for what to get my person either."

Jamie smiled. "I have an idea for mine."

"Me too." Billy nodded.

"Good," Jessie said. "Then you two can help me."

Jared stood up. "No one's allowed to help anyone else. You can do it, Jess. Try harder."

Billy held up his Bible. "I've been reading more of the Christmas story. It says the first gifts given to Jesus were gold, frankincense, and myrrh."

"Would my person like any of those gifts?" Jessie paused for a moment, then shook her head. "No. I don't think she would."

Jared glared at his sister.

Jessie covered her mouth with her hand. "Oops! Sorry."

"Knock it off, Jessie," Jared warned her. "Do you want to be part of this group or not?"

"All right. I'll stop. I promise." Jessie sat up straight and opened her Bible.

Rosie smiled. Jessie had said, "she." That narrowed it down even more. Jessie couldn't have Billy or his dad. And, since it was someone she barely knew, it must be Mrs. Wilson.

She wondered about the others. She guessed that Billy hadn't drawn his dad's name—but he and Jamie already had gift ideas, so they must have someone they knew well. She decided Billy had Grandma, and Jamie had Kristy.

"Who were these wise men in the book of Matthew?" Billy asked.

Billy's question took Rosie's thoughts away from the gifts. She wished she could stop trying to figure out who had who. It was making her a little crazy.

"They were kings," Jessie insisted. "You know, like in the song, 'We Three Kings of Orient Are.'"

"They weren't real kings," Lauren said.

"I don't think so either," Carrie added.

"Let's read the Bible and see what it says," Jared suggested. "Jessie, would you read from Matthew chapter 2?"

Jessie found the passage and began reading,

> *Now when Jesus was born in Bethlehem of Judaea in the days of Herod the king, behold, there came wise men from the east to Jerusalem,*
>
> *Saying, Where is he that is born King of the Jews? for we have seen his star in the east, and are come to worship him.*
>
> *When Herod the king had heard these things, he was troubled, and all Jerusalem with him.*
>
> *And when he had gathered all the chief priests and scribes of the people together, he demanded of them where Christ should be born.*
>
> *And they said unto him, In Bethlehem of Judaea: for thus it is written by the prophet,*
>
> *And thou Bethlehem, in the land of Juda, art not the least among the princes of Juda: for out of thee shall come a Governor, that shall rule my people Israel.*
>
> *Then Herod, when he had privily called the wise men, enquired of them diligently what time the star appeared.*
>
> *And he sent them to Bethlehem, and said, Go and search diligently for the young child; and when ye have found him, bring me word again, that I may come and worship him also.*
>
> *When they had heard the king, they departed; and, lo, the star, which they saw in the east, went before them, till it came and stood over where the young child was.*

When they saw the star, they rejoiced with exceeding great joy. And when they were come into the house, they saw the young child with Mary his mother, and fell down, and worshipped him: and when they had opened their treasures, they presented unto him gifts; gold, and frankincense and myrrh.

And being warned of God in a dream that they should not return to Herod, they departed into their own country another way.

Billy scratched his head. "I wish there were more details in these stories. Who were those guys? And how did they know about Jesus if they lived so far away?"

"If God had added all the details," Lauren said, "our Bibles would weigh about a hundred pounds and be too big for us to carry."

This was Billy's first Christmas as a believer, and he wanted to know all about it. Rosie knew none of them had answers for all of his questions. "Everyone, give me your questions. I'll write them down, and we can ask our parents later."

By the time they were finished, Rosie had compiled this list:

What was a "wise man?"

Were they kings?

How many were there?

Where did they come from?

How did they know about Jesus?

Was it a real star that guided the wise men?

Did they go to the stable?

Why did they give gold, frankincense, and myrrh to a baby?

Rosie couldn't remember when she hadn't known the Christmas story, but after writing down all the questions, she realized that she didn't fully understand it either.

8

First Drive

꒦

Rosie put on her cowboy hat and climbed into the cart while Grandma stood at Rascal's head, holding him by the bridle. The mild fall weather had provided plenty of opportunities to work with the ponies outdoors. They'd spent so long on the various training exercises, she had sometimes wondered if she would ever actually drive Rascal.

That day had finally arrived!

She scooted to the middle of the seat and gathered the reins in her hands. Rosie looked over Rascal's hindquarters and saw his furry ears flick backward to listen to what was going on behind him. He seemed to know that this day was different.

After getting herself situated, Rosie nodded to her grandmother. "Ready!"

When Grandma started walking, Rascal stepped forward, pulling into the harness.

Rosie smiled as the cart rolled gently over the sandy footing of the arena. She wasn't driving Rascal herself yet, but it was still exciting. "This is so cool!"

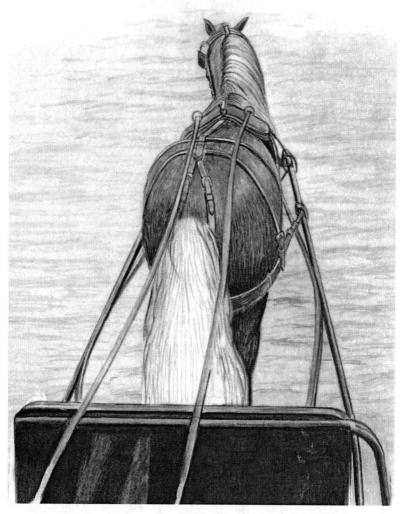

Grandma led the pony around the ring. He was used to Rosie being behind him from the ground driving and didn't seem frightened by the cart.

"Good boy, Rascal! You're doing great," Rosie reassured him.

After two laps, her grandmother let go of the reins. "You're on your own, Rosie! He seems fine, but I'll stay close in case he gets frightened."

"You can do it, Rosie!" Carrie stood beside their dad, watching from the side of the arena.

Rosie took a deep breath and clucked, signaling the pony to walk forward. She was finally driving! Rascal walked briskly, his head bobbing in time with his steps. "Good boy! I knew you could do it."

The cart bounced slightly as they moved along. When they reached the end of the arena, Rosie turned to the right and glanced at her dad and grandmother. "We're doing it!"

"Yay, Rascal!" Eric clapped. "I think it was my incredible training skills that got him to this point."

Rosie smiled at her dad. He was nearly as excited about this day as she was. It had been fun working with him to train the pony.

"Stay focused on Rascal!" Grandma called out to her. "But, yes, he's doing really well."

Rosie studied the pony in front of her, looking for any sign of fear or nervousness. She remembered the story about Ebony's wreck. That worried her a little, but Rascal didn't seem bothered by the cart.

Rosie had been impatient with their slow progress at first. She would have hooked Rascal up to the cart and started driving long before now, but the hours of preliminary training had paid off. Rascal was much calmer than when they'd begun. Of course, they were still in the arena, so there wasn't much to spook him.

"Rascal! We're actually driving!" She wanted to give him a big hug, but it was a long way from her seat in the cart to the pony's neck.

Rosie remembered the Amish boys at the auction. In some ways, she envied them. She'd like traveling around in a horse-drawn buggy. She couldn't wait to give cart rides to the children who visited Sonrise Stable. Rascal could be in parades too.

They circled the arena several more times, and then her Grandmother held Rascal's bridle while Rosie stepped out of the cart.

"That was excellent for the first time!" Eric patted Rascal and unhooked his cart.

Grandma agreed. "If he keeps doing that well, he'll make a fine little driving pony."

"You hear that, buddy?" Rosie rubbed his forehead. She led the pony outside the arena and tied him to a fence post. She removed his harness and set it on the floor of the cart her dad had wheeled out. While Rosie worked on Rascal, Grandma and Carrie finished harnessing Charley in the arena.

Rosie stood at Rascal's head to watch Carrie. Her grandmother walked Charley around the ring a few times, and then Carrie drove him on her own.

Carrie smiled broadly and waved when she drove past Rosie.

"Yay!" Rosie didn't yell, because she didn't want to frighten Charley. She pulled Rascal's head around so he faced the arena. "You're supposed to watch Charley, so you can see how to behave."

Rascal tossed his head and turned around to bite at a fly on his side.

"Rascal!" Rosie shook her head. "How are you going to learn if you don't pay attention?"

When Carrie was finished, she stopped next to where Rascal was tied. Rosie climbed through the fence to help her.

"Charley did so well," Carrie said. "I don't feel like I'm training him at all. He already seems to know everything I ask him to do."

"He might." Grandma helped the girls unhook Charley's cart. "When ponies get passed around to several owners, you don't always know what kind of training they've had. It won't hurt him to have a refresher course, though."

Despite what the previous owner had told them, Rosie was certain Rascal had never been driven before. He had taken longer than Charley to become comfortable at every step of the training.

"That was excellent for their first drives!" Grandma said. "We'll keep the sessions short at first and then gradually increase their driving time."

"Will they be ready for the nativity?" Rosie asked.

"We still have six weeks," Grandma said. "If you practice every day, they should be ready. We'll just have to see how they do."

Her grandmother's words reminded Rosie of her problem. Only six weeks until Christmas—and she still didn't have a single idea for Abigail's gift. Everyone had been quiet about the gift projects. She hadn't seen anything to give her a clue about what the others were working on.

The girls walked side by side, leading the ponies to the barn. Carrie tied Charley to the hitching rail so she could remove his harness. Since Rascal was already unharnessed, Rosie continued into the barn with him.

Abigail stood in the aisle with her back to them, brushing Raja. Rosie shoved Rascal into his stall and hurriedly shut the door hoping to avoid talking to her.

Abigail untied her horse from the crossties. "Still working with the little runt, I see."

Rosie swallowed and resolved to stay calm. "Rascal's not a runt. I'm getting him ready for the live nativity. Carrie and I are going to give kids rides in the pony carts."

Abigail walked down the aisle toward her. "What's a live nativity? Is there such a thing as a dead nativity?"

"That's not funny!" Rosie snapped. It was one thing to make fun of a pony, but she wouldn't let Abigail make fun of Jesus' birth.

"Chill out." Abigail frowned. "What are you so mad about?"

Did the girl really not know what a nativity was? Or was she playing some kind of game with her? "We're going to decorate the stable like a village in Bible times and act out the Christmas story."

"Oh…"

Rosie wasn't sure Abigail knew what she meant by the Christmas story, so she added, "When Jesus was born, I mean."

"Yeah." Abigail tossed her head. "I'm not the religious type."

Rosie sensed that God wanted her to invite Abigail to the nativity. That was about the last thing she wanted to do right then, but the longer she stood there, the stronger the feeling became. *Okay, God, if I have to.* "Do you want to come to it? It's going to be on Christmas Eve."

"Um, I think I have a party that night." Abigail walked toward the door. "Are you going to drive the other runt, Harley, too?"

"Charley!" Rosie yelled after her. "His name is Charley."

"I want to be Mary!" Jessie insisted.

"Now haven't we talked about that, honey?" Julie frowned at her daughter. "You're too young to play the part of Mary."

"And you're too short," Jared added.

Jessie's lip quivered as if she were about to cry.

"If the live nativity goes well," Julie said, "we'll do it every year. In a few years, you'll be tall enough to be Mary."

Jessie sat on the couch and leaned against her mother's side. "Who is going to be Mary then?"

"That's a good question," Grandma said. "We have a lot of females in the family, but it seems we're all either too old or too young."

"I don't know about Mary," Eric said, "but Billy's about the right age to be Joseph."

"Me?" Billy's eyes widened. "You're kidding, right?"

Eric shook his head. "No, I think you'd be perfect. The rest of us guys are too old."

"I'm not too old," Jared said, "but I am too short."

It was the middle of November, and they had gathered in the living room of the big farmhouse to finalize plans for the nativity.

Rosie liked the idea of Billy being Joseph.

"Abigail could be Mary," Jared suggested. "She's pretty tall."

Rosie gave him a look. What? Why was he always bringing her up? Abigail as Mary? She knew there wasn't much chance of that happening.

"We could ask her," Grandma agreed. "That would be a good way of witnessing to her."

Abigail was a year older than Rosie and Carrie, but she was taller and could easily pass for fifteen or sixteen. Rosie supposed it was all right to ask her. She knew Abigail would never agree to take the part.

"If she doesn't want to do it, I'm sure a girl from our homeschool group would be Mary," Kristy said.

"Maybe you could find someone in the group for Billy to marry," Jessie joked.

"Hey now," Billy said. "I'm not exactly ready to get married yet."

"Billy's a fine young man." Grandma smiled at him. "Someday God will bring the right young woman into his life."

Billy squirmed in his chair.

"Too mushy!" Jessie rolled her eyes.

Rosie stared at her. "You're the one who started it."

"All right, if we're finished arranging Billy's marriage, we need to get back to our nativity plans," Eric said.

"Yes. Please do," Billy laughed.

Grandma had written all the roles in a notebook. She started it around for everyone to sign up for how they wanted to help with the nativity.

When the notebook came to her, Rosie wrote her name down on the line next to "pony cart driver" and passed it on to Carrie. They would drive children from one scene to the next—that is, if the ponies were ready.

Rosie planned to drive Rascal every day until he was as steady and safe as an Amish buggy horse.

When the adults finished discussing their plans, Jared came over to Rosie. "Let's go to the barn and see if we can find Abigail. I hope she'll say yes."

Rosie followed Jared out of the house, hoping with each step she took, that Abigail would say no.

When they didn't find Abigail or Raja in the barn, they went outside to the riding arena. Abigail was cantering the Arabian around the ring. She rode past Jared and Rosie without even looking at them. After a few more laps, she stopped. "What? Why are you guys always spying on me?"

Spying on her? How could Abigail think that? Rosie tried to avoid her as much as possible.

Jared explained about their plans for the live nativity at Sonrise Stable.

"Yeah, so what? Rosie already told me about that."

Rosie stared at her. Did the girl find it impossible to be polite?

Jared wasn't phased by her rudeness. "We're missing someone for one of the most important parts. Would you like to be Mary?"

"You want me to be Mary?" Abigail laughed. "You mean the mother of Jesus, right?"

Rosie was surprised Abigail even knew who Mary was.

Jared nodded. "Yes."

"Why are you asking me?"

"We thought you'd be good at it," Jared said.

Rosie covered her mouth to hide a laugh. Did Jared honestly believe that? The truth was that they didn't have anyone else for the part, and Abigail's only qualification was her height.

"No." Abigail frowned. "Really, that's not my kind of thing."

Jared refused to give up. "Billy's going to be Joseph, but we don't have anyone to be Mary."

Abigail perked up at the mention of Billy's name. "He is?"

Oh, brother. The expression on her face confirmed what Rosie had suspected for a while. Abigail definitely had a crush on Billy. That was so ridiculous. Rosie was certain Billy had absolutely no interest in her.

"Okay. Sure, I'll do it! What should I wear? I have a sky-blue silk dress with a white lace collar that might be perfect."

Rosie shook her head. "Grandma's making costumes for everyone." Did Abigail think this was going to be a fashion show? Rosie had been a shepherd once in an outdoor nativity for their church. All she had thought about was getting enough clothes on under her costume to stay warm in the freezing weather.

"Will there be a lot of practices?"

Abigail obviously hoped there would be.

"Grandma and our parents are working out all the details," Jared said. "I'll let you know when we set the practice dates. They'll start after Thanksgiving."

Rosie couldn't stand to look at Abigail's starstruck face another minute. She turned to Raja. She was surprised Abigail still had him. Her father had talked about buying her another, more expensive horse, but maybe he had changed his mind after the trail riding incident.

It wasn't fair. Lauren wanted a horse so badly, and Abigail had a great one that she didn't appreciate.

9
The Lie

༺

"Wait for us!" Rosie clucked for Rascal to trot in order to catch up with Carrie and Charley. The pony became nervous when Charley got too far away, and Rosie didn't want him to panic. Rascal and Charley had been doing so well that the girls were allowed to drive them in the driveway and around the yard now as well as in the arena.

To make the driving practice more interesting, they were playing Follow the Leader, with each of them taking turns being the leader. Tick joined in the game, running and barking behind the carts. The big Rottweiler had provided some unanticipated additional training. At first, both ponies were leery of the dog chasing after them. It didn't take long, though, until they became accustomed to Tick barking and running around.

Carrie had coaxed the dog into her cart several times, but Tick didn't enjoy being a passenger. She only stayed in a few seconds before jumping out and resuming her own version of the cart game.

Charley had taken to driving so quickly that Rosie was a bit envious. With enough practice, she was convinced Rascal could be as good. She needed to be patient and keep working with him.

Carrie zigzagged down the arena and zipped out the gate.

"Come on, Rascal. You can do that." Rosie steered the pony back and forth, then trotted out the gate—just not as fast as Carrie had gone. She pulled up alongside her sister. "Let's stop for a minute. They need to practice standing still too."

While they rested, Rosie watched Rascal's sides move in and out with his rapid breathing. Tick lay down in the grass beside the drive, panting after all the running she had done. Rascal reached over to nudge Charley with his nose.

"Oh, no you don't!" Rosie pulled the pony's head back so he faced forward.

Grandma had warned them to keep the ponies far enough apart that they couldn't touch. If they rubbed against each other, parts of their harness might become entangled. Then when one of them tried to pull free, he'd pull against the other one. That could frighten both ponies and might cause a wreck. Rosie didn't want anything to happen to Rascal or Charley, so she made sure Rascal kept his nose to himself.

Tick suddenly jumped up and barked, moving protectively between the girls' carts.

"Who's that?" Carrie pointed down the path that led to the woods.

Rosie squinted. "I can't tell. They're too far away."

Tick trotted off to investigate while the girls sat and watched.

"It's Billy," Rosie said as the figure came closer. "What in the world is he doing?"

"Get up, Rascal." Rosie clucked to the pony and steered him toward the path where Billy approached on Sassy.

Carrie drove Charley beside them. "Sassy's pulling something."

"Hey!" Rosie called out.

Billy waved. "Hey yourself!"

When they came close enough, Rosie could see that Billy had a long rope wrapped around Sassy's saddle horn. The other end was attached to a thick, four-foot long log the mule was dragging. Tick ran from one side of the log to the other, barking and snapping at it.

When he was even with them, Billy stopped. "What's the matter? You've never seen a mule work before? They're actually useful animals, you know."

"Yeah, I know that," Rosie said. "But why are you dragging that log around?"

Billy grinned. "Sassy's been putting on weight, so I thought this might be good exercise for her. You know, slim her down a bit."

She rolled her eyes. "Very funny. Now seriously, what are you doing?"

"This log was down across one of our trails—"

"And," Rosie finished Billy's sentence, "you fell in love with it and had to bring it home with you?"

"Kind of," Billy played along, "but it was Sassy who fell in love with it. I couldn't get her away from the log, so there was nothing I could do but lasso it and bring it home for her." Billy nodded to the girls and signaled the mule to walk. Tick tried to pounce on the log again once it was in motion.

Rosie yelled out to Billy, "You and that mule are both crazy!"

Billy waved, but didn't turn around.

Rosie and Carrie followed him to the barn.

Billy rode over to his old, beat-up truck, dropped the rope, and dismounted. "You girls want to help me lift this into my truck?"

"You're kidding, right?" Rosie glanced at the log. "That thing weighs more than Carrie and me combined."

"Why don't you put it in Sassy's stall since she loves it so much?" Carrie said.

Billy shook his head. "You've been hanging around your sister too much. You're starting to sound just like her."

Rosie laughed. "I don't advise putting that log in your truck anyway. That old thing might fall apart."

Billy put a hand on each side of the mule's head and looked into her large brown eyes. "What am I going to do, Sassy? These two little goofballs are driving me crazy!"

Sassy rubbed her big head against Billy's side nearly knocking him into the truck. "Hey now, none of that."

Billy pushed the mule away and released the latch to lower the tailgate at the back of his truck, but the tailgate fell off. He stood and stared at it lying on the ground. "I need to fix that thing someday."

Rosie laughed. "See! What did I tell you? Your truck would never hold that log. Why don't you drag it out to the arena? I could practice jumping Scamper over it."

"Since that pony arrived," Billy pointed to Rascal, "you don't even ride Scamper."

"Yes, I do," Rosie insisted. "I had to work with Rascal a lot so he'd be ready for the nativity." Billy's comment worried her. Did Scamper think she had abandoned him? Since Rascal was doing so well now, she'd have more time to spend with Scamper.

Billy untied the rope from the log, coiled it, and threw it behind the seat of his truck. "When are we practicing for that thing?"

"The nativity? No one's decided yet," Rosie said. "Did you hear Abigail agreed to be Mary?"

Billy's eyes widened. "I thought you said she wouldn't do it."

Rosie shrugged. "Surprised me!"

"Me too," Carrie said.

"Is your dad around?" Billy asked. "I really do need some help getting this into my truck."

"He might be up at the house," Carrie said.

"Where are you taking that thing?" Rosie asked.

"To my dad's. He loves logs too."

"You must have inherited it from him," Rosie laughed. "Come on, Carrie. Let's go practice driving some more."

By the time the girls returned from practicing with Rascal and Charlie, the log and Billy's truck were both gone. They tied the ponies to the hitching post.

Grandma came out of the back porch and went over to help them. "I was about to come and get you two. You're going to wear the legs off those ponies, driving them so much."

Rosie bent down and checked Rascal. "It's okay. His legs are still there!"

Grandma laughed and helped unharness the pony.

When they had trained Scamper, her grandmother had told Rosie it took a lot of wet saddle blankets to make a good horse. She figured the more she drove Rascal, the better he would be.

When they were finished, Rosie led Rascal into the barn. She met Abigail carrying hay to Raja.

Abigail didn't bother to say hi. "Have you set the first nativity practice yet?"

"Um, no."

When Rascal tried to grab a bite of Raja's hay, Abigail jerked the flake away from him. "Stay back, you little thief! This is for *my* horse."

Rosie glared at Abigail. As she pulled Rascal's head back, a thought suddenly came to her. She looked around to make sure Carrie was still outside with Grandma, then said, "Billy might not be able to be Joseph—something about maybe starting college. My parents are waiting to set the first practice date until he makes a decision. 'Cause if he goes, we'll have to find someone else to be Joseph—Jared might do it."

Rosie couldn't believe she had told such a lie. But it made her angry that Abigail only wanted the part of Mary so she could be with Billy—and the girl's rude behavior annoyed her.

"What?" Abigail turned suddenly toward Rosie. "Billy's going to college? I didn't know that."

"No." Rosie shook her head. "Not many people know about it yet." *Yeah, not even Billy.*

"I wonder which school he's going to. I'll have to ask him about it the next time I see him."

Rosie's eyes widened. "Oh! No. Please, don't say anything about it. He wants to keep it quiet until he makes up his mind. I shouldn't have said anything about it to you." *That was the truth.* "Um, I have to go help Carrie."

She hurried to put Rascal in his stall, then ran out of the barn. Grandma was still helping Carrie with Charley. Rosie picked up a brush and began grooming the pony. What if Abigail asked Billy about going to college? Surely, the girl would tell everyone that she had lied to her, and then she'd be in big trouble. Rosie brushed the same spot on Charley's shoulder repeatedly. Her punishment would be less if she told the truth. She took a deep breath and decided to get it over with. "Grandma?"

Her grandmother set a piece of the harness on the ground.

"Grandma?" Rosie repeated.

"What?" She still didn't turn around.

"I kind of told a lie a few minutes ago," Rosie said quietly.

Grandma stood and faced her. "Kind of? It's hard to 'kind of' tell a lie. Either you told a lie or you didn't."

Rosie couldn't look at her or Carrie. She stared at the ground. "I did."

Grandma removed Charley's bridle. "I'm surprised at you, Rosie. What did you lie about?"

"I told Abigail that Billy might be going to college."

Her grandmother coughed a few times.

Rosie raised her head. Was Grandma choking—or trying not to laugh?

"Why in the world did you say that?" Grandma said when she finally caught her breath.

"It's not right! She only wants to be Mary so she can hang around with Billy."

Grandma's expression softened. "I agree; it's not a good reason, but God may use the experience to teach her something anyway. It might be the first time she's heard the real story of Christmas. I'll keep an eye on her, but you don't need to worry about it anymore."

"Am I in trouble?"

"I imagine so." Grandma nodded. "Go talk to your mom or dad."

Rosie walked toward the house, trying to decide which of her parents she'd rather face. Getting back at Abigail wasn't worth feeling as miserable as she did right now. Next time, she'd think before she let something so stupid pop out of her mouth.

10

A Drive to the Woods

L et's go back to the woods today," Carrie suggested when they finished their barn chores.

It was unusually warm for late November, and Rosie was comfortable in just a hooded sweatshirt. The leaves had fallen from the trees, and everything was turning brown in preparation for another cold Ohio winter. Rosie loved early fall with its summer-like temperatures and colorful leaves, but the dull drabness of late fall made her eager for a big snow to cover all the brown.

They had a little more than four weeks before the live nativity, and the girls wanted to get in as much practice with the ponies as they could.

Rosie had put the harness on so many times that the process was as familiar to her as saddling Scamper. When Rascal was harnessed, she carefully positioned the end of the reins over the cart seat and sat on them, an extra safety measure her grandmother had taught the girls.

The path to the woods was too narrow to drive side by side, so Carrie went first with Charley since he was the calmer of the two ponies.

A cool breeze blew through Rosie's hair. She glanced up at the overcast sky. "Do you think it's ever going to snow?"

Their dad had purchased sleigh runners for both carts, and Rosie couldn't wait to try them out. All they had to do was remove the wheels and pop the runners on in their place to convert the two carts into sleighs. If only it would snow!

"Not today!" Carrie spoke loudly so she didn't have to turn around. "It must be close to fifty degrees out here."

This was probably more like Bethlehem weather at this time of year, but Rosie was used to it being cold and snowy by now. Anyway, it had been perfect for training the ponies outdoors.

Rosie was pleased with how well Rascal was behaving. Maybe he'd turn out to be a Jeremiah after all. Grandma was keeping an eye out for a pony wagon with a double hitch so they could drive Rascal and Charley together. The ponies would look good together as a team.

As they entered the woods, Rosie jerked at a sudden crashing sound in the brush on their left. "What was that?"

She couldn't see anything, but Rascal had heard it too. The pony froze in his tracks. He flung his head upward and turned in the direction of the noise.

"Easy, boy." Rosie gripped the reins tightly and pulled back.

A deer leaped through the brush onto the trail ahead of Charley. Rosie let out the breath she had been holding. There were deer all over their farm. Rascal probably saw them all the time when he was in the pasture. He wouldn't be afraid of that.

After the deer moved on, Carrie started Charley walking again.

Rosie signaled Rascal to follow. He started forward with a prancing step. "Nothing to worry about, buddy, it was only a—"

CRACK!

Rosie jumped at the loud sound of a gunshot. Rascal jigged to the right, then to the left, trying to pass Charley. Rosie pulled on the reins to make him stand still. Why was someone shooting on their property? She glanced to her left in the direction of the sound, but didn't see anyone. Her heart thumped. That sounded close! Who was out in their woods with a gun?

CRACK!

The second shot was louder than the first. Rascal reared and whirled to the right, tipping the cart dangerously. Rosie grabbed the metal frame at the edge of the seat and held on. Before the wheel touched the ground again, the pony took off at a gallop. Once out of the woods, Rascal dispensed with the trail, taking the straightest course back toward the safety of the barn. He ran across a field rutted with deep hoofprints and tractor tires and thick with tall grass and weeds. The cart careened so wildly that Rosie felt herself bouncing up off the seat.

"Whoa, Rascal! Whoa!" She pulled back hard on the reins, but Rascal didn't even seem to notice. There was no stopping the pony right now. She held the reins in one hand and gripped the cart seat firmly with the other. Maybe after Rascal ran awhile, he'd tire enough that she'd be able to stop him.

"Rascal, please stop!" Rosie wondered briefly whether Carrie was all right. There was no way she could turn to look behind her. It was taking all her strength just to stay in the cart. *God, please help me stop him!*

A hundred feet ahead was a large hole where an old drain tile had washed out. It was surrounded by tall weeds. Did Rascal see it? "Whoa, boy! You have to stop!" If the pony stepped in the hole at this speed, he would surely break a leg. Rosie pulled until her arms ached, but Rascal didn't slow his pace.

As they came closer to the hole, Rosie let go of the reins and crouched forward, preparing to jump. Rascal swerved suddenly to the left. The cart tipped so steeply that she lost her grip and found herself flying out of it. "Oomph!" She landed on her right side with a thud and watched helplessly as the pony raced on without her. The cart righted itself and was still attached when Rascal disappeared from her sight.

Rosie found herself in a patch of weeds that had somewhat cushioned her fall. She wiped a clump of mud from her cheek. She twisted her head from side to side and lifted her arms. They felt fine, but when she tried to sit up, a sharp pain stabbed at her side and knocked her down. She rolled carefully onto her back and lay still for a moment, not daring to breathe. When forced to take another breath, Rosie felt the pain pierce her side again. Something was terribly wrong. Shallow breaths made the pain more bearable.

Rosie was nearly paralyzed by a sudden terrible thought. *Oh no!* Fear crept into her chest and squeezed at her heart, causing a pain worse than the one in her side. Carrie had been ahead of her at the entrance to the woods when the shots were fired. *What if…*

No! She wouldn't allow her thoughts to go there. *God, please don't let Carrie be hurt.*

She wanted to get up and find out what had happened to her sister, but another attempt at rising to a sitting position resulted in the same searing pain. Rosie lay motionless for several minutes, staring at the gray sky.

Why didn't someone come? They had to have heard the shots— her mom, dad, Grandma, anyone. She listened carefully but heard nothing, except the tall dead weeds shaking in the breeze.

Then she heard Carrie's voice.

"Rosie! Rosie!"

Tears welled up in her eyes when she heard her sister calling her name. Carrie was all right!

Charley stopped beside her, and Carrie leaped out of the cart. She dropped the reins, and the pony stood obediently. Carrie hurried to Rosie's side but remained standing as if afraid of what she might see if she came too close. "Oh, Rosie! Are you all right?"

"No." Rosie brushed away the tears that dripped from her eyes. "Get Mom and Dad!" There was much more she wanted to say, but talking was too painful.

"Hold still." Carrie held her palm out and backed up. "Don't move. I'll go get help." She bumped into the cart behind her and jumped onto the seat. "Get up, Charley!"

Don't move? There wasn't any danger of that happening. It was too painful even to sit up. The cart squeaked as Carrie started off. Rosie didn't try to watch them leave.

Oh, Rascal, why did you have to run away like that? She hoped the pony had made it back to the barn unharmed.

CRACK!

Rosie flinched at the sound of another shot. Who was in their woods? She hoped they wouldn't come any closer.

The cold from the ground crept through Rosie's sweatshirt into her back and seemed to seep into every bone in her body. She had never felt so cold.

Why was it taking so long for someone to come? It scared Rosie that it hurt so much to breathe. What if she had poked a hole in her lungs? Would they collapse so she couldn't breathe at all? She closed her eyes and prayed some more.

"Rosie!"

"Mom!"

Soon her mother was at her side, kissing her forehead. "How do you feel?"

Rosie's eyes filled with tears. "Awful."

"I'm so sorry, honey! I never should have let you two go out alone with those ponies."

"Wasn't his fault," Rosie communicated with as few words as possible. She didn't want Rascal blamed for the accident.

"Shh! I know. Carrie told us all about it."

"Rascal okay?"

"Yes. He's frightened, but not injured. Billy caught him as he came flying up to the barn."

Rosie smiled weakly.

"Don't talk. Your dad's at the house waiting for the ambulance so he can show them how to get back here."

"Grandma?"

"Shh," Kristy reminded her. "She's in town. She'll meet us at the hospital."

Rosie shivered. "Cold."

Kristy quickly unzipped her jacket and spread it over Rosie like a blanket.

Her mother's scent on the jacket was comforting, but Rosie still felt as if she were frozen to the ground.

Kristy held Rosie's hand and stroked her hair. "You'll be all right."

The blare of a siren grew louder as an emergency vehicle approached. Rather than making Rosie feel better, the sound frightened her. Tears dripped from the corners of her eyes.

Kristy squeezed her hand. "It's okay, honey. Help is almost here."

The ambulance bounced across the field and stopped beside them. Kristy backed up to join Eric, who walked behind the vehicle.

Two medics hurried toward Rosie, carrying a long board with holes at each side for handles. The men set the board on the ground and asked several questions about how she felt and where she was hurt. Rosie pointed, nodded, or shook her head to answer as many of the questions as possible without speaking.

After it seemed that they were finished examining her, the shorter man knelt and looked intently into Rosie's eyes.

When she saw his serious expression, Rosie worried that there *was* something dreadfully wrong with her.

"The last thing I need to know—" he leaned in closer, "is where you got your driver's license."

Rosie smiled. It hurt too much to laugh. Maybe she was going to be all right after all. He wouldn't be telling jokes if there was anything seriously wrong.

He smiled back. "We're going to move you into our limousine now. You ever ridden in one of these?"

Rosie liked the man's sparkly blue eyes and his sense of humor. She shook her head.

One man held her shoulders while the other gently lifted her legs. They slid her onto the board. Then they picked her up, board and all, and walked to the ambulance.

Kristy and Eric climbed in the back to ride with her. Soon the vehicle began to move slowly over the rough ground. Rosie winced at every jolt.

"Oh, honey, I wish I could take the pain away." Kristy squeezed Rosie's arm. "Once we get out of this field and onto the road, it won't hurt so much."

Rosie lay still and tried not to think about the pain. *Oh, Rascal, you ruined everything.*

11

Billy and Sassy

Carrie and Billy stood by the barn and watched the ambulance travel slowly down the driveway toward the road.

Carrie thought she could see her mom and dad through the windows. She fought back tears. "What do you think is wrong with Rosie? She didn't seem to be able to move. You don't think she's paralyzed, do you?"

"I don't know."

The somber look on Billy's face didn't make Carrie feel any better.

"We'll know more after they get to the hospital." Billy pulled a phone out of his back pocket and checked to make sure it was working. "Your dad said he'd text me as soon as they know something."

When Rascal had run up to the barn without Rosie, Billy tied him to the hitching post, then ran to find Eric.

"Come on; let's take care of these ponies." Billy began to unharness Rascal.

Carrie's hands were still shaky as she pulled the last piece of harness off Charley's back. "When we heard the gunshots, Rascal took off galloping. By the time I got Charley turned around, we couldn't catch them. I didn't see Rosie fall out of the cart." Carrie wiped her eyes on the sleeve of her jacket. "I hope she's not hurt too bad."

"I'm sure she'll be all right." Billy patted Carrie's head awkwardly.

Carrie took off Charley's bridle and slipped the halter onto his head. They led the ponies into the barn and put them in a stall together.

Billy closed the door and latched it. "Can you help me get all the horses in the barn?"

Carrie wondered why Billy wanted to bring them all in—and then she heard another gunshot. The sound wasn't as loud as it had been when she and Rosie were at the woods, but it still made her jump. "I see what you mean!"

She ran to open the sliding door at the back of the riding arena while Billy went out to the corral and herded the horses behind the barn.

When they had them all safely inside, Billy slid the large door shut and turned to Carrie. "I'm going out there to find out who's hunting on our property. There are 'No Trespassing' signs posted all over the place. No one should be in the woods."

Carrie couldn't believe she had heard him right. "You can't do that, Billy! You were worried about our horses—what about you? You might get shot out there!"

"Don't worry." Billy waved his hand at her. "I'll be careful. The sheriff can't do anything to him if I don't find out who he is. The guy doesn't know that he caused Rosie to be hurt."

Carrie wanted to see the person punished too, but she didn't want anything to happen to Billy. And she didn't want to be alone at the house with a stranger roaming around Sonrise Stable.

Billy caught Sassy and saddled the mule. "Go up to the house, Carrie. Your mom asked Julie to come and stay with you. She'll be here any minute. I need to get out there before that guy gets away."

Carrie stood and stared at Billy. He walked Sassy out of the barn, and then he swung up onto the mule without putting his foot in the stirrup.

Even though she was worried, Carrie had to smile. She and Rosie would have to try mounting that way some time. Her smile faded. That is—if Rosie wasn't seriously injured. Her sister just had to be all right!

After he'd ridden a few steps toward the trail that led to the woods, Billy twisted in the saddle to look at Carrie. "Go on inside. Keep Tick in the house. No one's going to mess with that big Rott."

Carrie couldn't believe Billy was going into the woods when there was a crazy man with a gun out there, but she knew she couldn't make him change his mind. She hoped Julie would arrive soon.

"Be careful, Billy!" Carrie turned and ran as fast as she could to the house.

It was nearly midnight by the time they arrived home from the hospital. Rosie felt like a toddler learning to walk as she took baby steps up onto the porch. Her mom was on one side of her and her dad on the other. Grandma hurried to open the front door.

Carrie rushed to Rosie's side as they entered the house. "Are you okay? Aunt Julie said you had two broken ribs."

Rosie grimaced and nodded.

Carrie's eyes widened. "That sounds awful."

"It feels awful."

Kristy and Eric steered her to the recliner in the living room. Rosie put both hands behind her and backed up. When she felt her hands touch the chair, she slowly lowered herself into it and leaned back.

"Lisa was working in the ER when we arrived at the hospital," Kristy said. "I think we all felt a little better when we saw her."

"What did they do for her?" Julie asked. "Does she have her ribs wrapped?"

"No. Apparently they don't do that anymore." Kristy held out several sheets of paper. "We have all kinds of instructions. Pain medicine every four hours. She'll sleep in the recliner for a few days, since lying down and getting up will be painful for a while."

"She has breathing exercises," Eric added. "Breathing expands the lungs, which pushes the ribs out. That hurts, but if she doesn't breathe deeply enough, she could get pneumonia."

"Oh, poor Rosie." Carrie's face clouded over as if she might cry.

It felt weird to have everyone talking about her as if she wasn't there, but it hurt so much to speak, that Rosie didn't object. "How's Rascal?"

"He wasn't hurt," Carrie said. "He broke his bridle and the reins, but the cart is fine."

Rosie smiled. That was a relief. The pony would have been fine if it weren't for the gunshots. He even stood pretty still for the first one.

"I'd love to get my hands on the guy who was in our woods," Eric muttered.

"Um…" Billy stepped forward from the back of the room.

"Billy!" Rosie stared at his face. What had happened to him?

Billy ran his hand across his forehead, partially covering a black eye. "I found the hunter."

"Are you crazy?" Grandma gasped. "You could have been shot!"

"Yeah, I guess I didn't think that through too well. I was so mad about what happened to Rosie; I didn't want him to get away without being punished."

"How did you end up with a black eye?" Eric asked.

"When I found him. . ." Billy scratched his head. "Hmm. I forget the exact words I used, but it was something like, 'What kind of idiot hunts on someone's property without their permission?'"

"Oh, Billy." Grandma shook her head. "I can't believe you did that."

"Tell me about it," Billy said. "Then I got off Sassy and walked over and demanded that he give me his name and phone number."

"Did he give it to you?" Kristy asked.

Billy frowned. "No. That's when he hauled off and hit me. He did it so fast; I didn't have time to defend myself. Then he took off running. My eye was watering so badly I couldn't see anything or else I would have chased him."

Listening to Billy's story made Rosie's eyes water. She blinked a few times. That must have really hurt. She couldn't believe Billy had done that for her. It was a good thing he hadn't been able to chase the man. His skinny frame was great for running, but if it came to fighting, he wouldn't have been a match for any good-sized man.

Grandma stepped closer to examine him. "Are you sure you're all right? When Lisa gets off work at the hospital, she could come over and check that eye."

"Nah." Billy shrugged away her offer. "I'm all right."

"I've had him putting ice on it off and on," Julie said.

Billy pulled a piece of paper out of his pocket. He grinned and waved it back and forth. "What the guy didn't know was that I had his license plate number!"

"How did you get that?" Eric took the paper and patted him on the back. "This is great!"

"I thought he must have parked somewhere outside the woods, so the first thing I did was take off on Sassy around the edge. Sure enough, at the back of our property not far from Lisa and Robert's cabin was a truck with an empty gun rack in the back window. I'm sure it's his. I've never seen anyone parked back there before."

Rosie noticed that Billy had said "our property." He did seem like one of the family. She hadn't gotten to have Gabe as her little brother, but it felt good to have Billy as a sort-of big brother.

Eric smiled. "Good job, Billy! I'll talk to the sheriff tomorrow and see what can be done about this."

"Sassy the Super Mule strikes again!" Carrie said.

"Yeah, it would have taken me way too long to walk all the way around there on foot," Billy said. "I couldn't have done it without the Super Mule."

"But," Grandma frowned, "that crazy hunter might have mistaken Sassy for a deer and shot both of you. You're fortunate you came out of this with only a black eye."

"Yeah, I guess so." Billy suddenly grew serious. "I've been thinking tonight while we were waiting on you guys to get home. With everything that's happened over the past year—Grandma and Carrie getting hurt, and now Rosie . . ."

Rosie didn't know what Billy was getting at. It was unusual to see him so serious.

"I want to become a paramedic so I can help people who are injured."

"Oh Billy! That's a wonderful idea," Grandma said.

"You'll make a great paramedic," Eric added.

"I don't know how to become one, though. Does anyone know what I have to do?"

"I can help you check into it tomorrow," Grandma said.

Rosie remembered the men who had helped her. She could picture Billy doing that. Would he have to leave Sonrise Stable, though? She shifted in the recliner trying to get comfortable and groaned when she felt the now familiar pain in her side.

"Is your pain getting worse?" Kristy checked her watch. "Let me get a glass of water. You're due for another pill."

Carrie sat on the floor in front of Rosie. "How long will it be until your ribs are healed?"

Rosie frowned. "Six weeks."

"Six weeks until you're fully healed," Grandma reminded her. "The doctor said you'd start to feel better in a couple of weeks."

She nodded slowly. Two weeks or six; it didn't matter. Everything was ruined. With only four weeks left until Christmas, there was no

101

way she could retrain Rascal in time for the live nativity. And she still didn't have a gift for Abigail. How was she supposed to get anything for her now that she had to stay inside for several weeks?

Rosie didn't want to think about it anymore. She swallowed the medicine her mother handed her, lay back in the recliner, and closed her eyes.

12

Horse Sketches

For the first few days after the accident, everyone in the family took turns staying inside with Rosie. Normally, lying around the house would be the last thing she wanted to do, but getting up and down and walking were so painful that she was content to spend most of the time resting in the recliner. The doctor insisted that she walk inside every day to prevent fluid from building up in her lungs. She was amazed at how even a short walk tired her now.

On Billy's next turn sitting with her, he was barely in the room before he started talking about paramedic programs. "First I have to become an EMT. That means emergency medical technician. It takes six months to finish that course."

Rosie nodded occasionally as she listened.

"Then I have to pass a state test. I'm not good at taking tests, so hopefully it won't be too hard."

"We can all help you study, Billy." Rosie wished he could start the program right away. She could help him study while she was stuck indoors.

"When I get a job and have worked as an EMT for six months, I'll start studying to become a paramedic." Billy frowned. "That program takes two years to complete."

"That might be what Abigail meant when she asked me about college last week." He shook his head. "But how could she have known about it, since I just decided to do this a few days ago?"

Rosie hurried to change the subject. She didn't want to explain about the lie she had told Abigail. "Your eye looks worse than ever. It's green, black, and blue. Very creepy."

"Yeah, it does look pretty bad. It doesn't hurt any more, though. It should start getting better soon. There aren't too many more colors it could turn into."

Rosie smiled. Billy seemed a little proud of his black eye. "I'm glad you got the license plate number. Dad said the sheriff knew exactly who the guy was."

"Yeah, I guess they've had problems with him trespassing before. I don't think he'll bother us again."

Rosie was happy for Billy, but she knew that once he began taking classes, he wouldn't have as much time to help at Sonrise Stable. That made her sad at the same time. "You'll be a great paramedic."

"I hope so. Oh, yeah. I forgot this part! Your dad gave me information about a mounted rescue unit not far from here. I'm going to join that group. That way Sassy can be involved too."

"What do they do?" Rosie enjoyed listening to Billy talk about his plans. She'd never seen him this excited about anything before.

"It's a group that helps find people who are lost in the forest and stuff like that. You know—remote areas they can't get vehicles into."

"Sassy the Super Mule will be good at that."

Billy nodded. "They have a training program Sassy and I have to complete."

When her dad had first brought the mule home, Rosie had disliked her instantly. She couldn't believe how wrong she had been about Sassy. Come to think of it, she hadn't liked Billy at first either. Maybe she was wrong about Abigail too. She'd have to try harder to get along with her.

"You're going to be busy, Billy."

"Yeah. I'll have to pay for my classes somehow, so I need to keep working here as much as I can."

Rosie looked around the living room. "Remember when you came here to help Dad fix up our house?"

"This place was a mess! I thought your family was crazy to buy it. Everyone who lives around here thought it was a haunted house."

"I was so mad when Dad asked you to work here."

Billy grinned. "I do seem to remember that."

"Now I don't want you to leave." Rosie felt tears welling up in her eyes.

"Aw, I'm not going anywhere right away." Billy patted her on the head. "Except back out to the barn. I still have to work with that colt of yours today."

Billy was training Majestic, the nurse mare foal Grandma had adopted from the Last Chance Corral.

"How's Majestic doing?"

"He's a smart boy. He lunges both directions now and responds to voice commands to walk and trot."

Rosie could tell Billy loved that part of his job. He was becoming a very good horse trainer. Maybe he could help her with her pony too. "How's Rascal?"

Billy stood and put on his jacket. "See ya later, kid." He slipped out the front door as Carrie came in to take his place.

Carrie took off her coat and boots and sat on the couch, pulling a blanket up around her. "Charley had a great drive today."

Rosie nodded glumly.

Carrie's smile faded until it matched Rosie's expression. "I can't wait until you can come outside again."

Rosie couldn't wait either, but right now, she found it challenging enough to get in and out of the recliner.

"If I'd been driving Rascal when the guy was shooting in the woods, I would have totally freaked out. Charley's so easy to drive."

Rosie sighed. "Grandma had told me to pull on one rein, then the other if Rascal tried to run off. But when he was galloping and the cart was bouncing around so crazily, I totally forgot about it. I just kept pulling back on both reins. It was my fault he got away from me."

"It wasn't your fault," Carrie assured her. "If anything, it was my fault. It was my idea to go to the woods that day. If I hadn't suggested that, none of this would have happened."

"Now I won't be able to drive Rascal for the nativity." Poor Rascal. As soon as Rosie could go to the barn again, she'd work out a plan with Grandma to retrain the pony.

"We can share Charley if you feel better by then," Carrie offered.

"Thanks. Has Grandma said when we can start over with Rascal?"

Carrie shrugged. "I don't know."

Rosie sat quietly for a moment. She was determined to work with Rascal to make him a good driving pony, but that was a future project. What could she do *now*? Suddenly she had an inspiration. "Carrie, would you get my drawing tablet and pencils?"

"Sure." Carrie jumped off the couch and ran upstairs. She returned and handed the art supplies to her sister.

Rosie opened the tablet to the first blank page and selected a drawing pencil. It had just occurred to her what to make for Abigail's Christmas gift—a booklet of horse sketches. And each page would have one of Rosie's favorite Bible verses.

Picking Abigail's name had put a damper on Christmas for Rosie, and her attitude had gotten worse as the weeks passed. Now that she finally had an idea for her gift, she was excited about Operation Christmas Spirit.

106

Her sister was sitting right next to her, but Rosie drew all the time, so Carrie wouldn't suspect anything. The Bible verses and a cover could be added later when no one was around.

She'd make this book the best that she could. Rosie smiled and began to draw. The first picture was going to be Abigail's Arabian, Raja.

13

Wise Men

In the week since her driving accident, Rosie had progressed from the recliner to the living room couch, but she hadn't ventured outside yet. Since she wasn't able to make it to the Bible study in the activity barn, the kids brought the study to her. In fact, Grandma, her mom, and both aunts had joined them this time.

When everyone was seated, Rosie opened her Bible to the second chapter of the book of Matthew. She followed along as her grandmother began reading. "Now when Jesus was born in Bethlehem of Judaea in the days of Herod the king, behold, there came wise men from the east to Jerusalem—"

"Where is He—" a deep voice boomed out.

Rosie jumped a little. Three men in long robes entered the room.

"Where is He that is born King of the Jews?" Eric continued, speaking in a loud, deeper-than-usual voice. He looked around as if he were searching for the baby Jesus right there in the living room.

Robert stood beside Eric and pointed to the window. "For we have seen His star in the east and are come to worship Him."

Jonathan joined them carrying a gold box. "We have brought Him gifts of gold, frankincense, and myrrh."

The three men wore long, flowing robes—purple, blue, and red, with gold and silver trim, matching hats, and long beards.

"Whoa! Impressive! You guys look like the real thing," Billy said.

If Rosie hadn't known her dad was going to be a wise man in the live nativity, she might not have recognized him. "Grandma, did you make those costumes? They're amazing!"

Her grandmother smiled. "It took a while, but they did turn out nicely, didn't they?"

Rosie nodded. "They sure did!"

"Where are your camels?" Jessie asked.

"I'm afraid we couldn't locate any camels," Julie said. "The wise men may have actually ridden horses anyway. We don't know for sure, but *these* wise men will definitely arrive on horseback."

"Good," Eric laughed. "I've never ridden a camel in my life."

"You can ride Scamper, Dad," Rosie offered. "He's been neglected, since I spent so much time training Rascal. And now I can't go to the barn at all."

"Thanks," Eric said. "I'll get him out this afternoon and start practicing. It wouldn't be good for one of the wise men to fall off his horse."

The wise men pulled up chairs and arranged their robes so they could sit down.

"Now," Eric said, "I hear you have some questions for us."

Rosie smiled. This should be interesting, learning about the wise men from "real" wise men. "Were you kings? What exactly was a wise man?"

"We only know for certain what is stated in the Bible," Grandma reminded them, "and as you've discovered, there aren't many details in that story. Our wise men will try to answer your questions, but they'll just be educated guesses."

Eric pulled off his beard and hat and set them on the coffee table. "Some call us kings, but the word in the Greek is *magoi*, which is translated magi."

"We are part of a group of wise, learned men who study signs in the heavens," Jonathan added. "That's how the magi noticed the special star."

"We come from a country in the east, probably Persia," Robert said.

"Were there three of you?" Jessie walked up to her father and rubbed her hand over the sleeve of his costume.

Jonathan pulled her onto his lap. "Some say there were three of us because of the three gifts. The Bible doesn't give a number, though. It only indicates that there was more than one."

"What I don't understand," Billy said, "is how the wise men knew to search for a star in the first place. How did they know that Jesus would be born?"

That was a good question. Rosie hadn't thought about that before, but she knew her dad would have a good explanation.

"Long ago, the Jewish people who lived in Judah were taken captive to the country of Babylon," Eric explained. "Among them was a young Hebrew named Daniel. The Babylonian king, Nebuchadnezzar, had an unusual dream that none of his magi were able to interpret. Nebuchadnezzar was about to put all those wise men to death. Apparently they weren't so wise, if they couldn't tell the king what his dream meant! But when Daniel was called in, he was able to give the correct meaning of the dream. The wise men's lives were saved, and the king appointed Daniel as the ruler over all the magi."[1]

Robert picked up from there. "It's thought that Daniel taught those magi the Old Testament prophecies of a coming Savior, including Numbers 24:17, given by Balaam: 'there shall come a Star out of Jacob, and a Sceptre shall rise out of Israel.' Those Hebrew teachings were passed down to other magi over the years."

1   Daniel 2:48

"Ah, that kind of makes sense," Billy said. "I'm reading the New Testament for the first time. I'll study the Old Testament next."

"What did the star look like?" Jamie asked. "How did you know it was a special star?"

"The Bible says the wise men saw not just *a* star, but *His* star in the east, so there was definitely something different about it," Eric said. "They recognized it as a sign of the Christ's birth. It seems they didn't see the star again until they left Herod's palace: 'When they had heard the king, they departed; and, lo, the star, which they saw in the east, went before them, till it came and stood over where the young child was.'"[2]

"That's unusual behavior for a star," Robert added. "One of my favorite Bible teachers, John MacArthur, believes it wasn't a physical star, but the Shekinah glory of God."

Jessie turned to look at her dad. "What's that?"

"The Shekinah glory was the cloudy pillar that guided the Israelites as they escaped from slavery in Egypt and wandered in the wilderness," Eric said. "It went before them and led the way, which is exactly what the 'star' did for the wise men. The Shekinah glory may have appeared to the shepherds also: 'And, lo, the angel of the Lord came upon them, and the *glory* of the Lord shone round about them: and they were sore afraid.'"[3]

"That would explain why more people didn't see the star and go see Jesus," Jonathan said. "When they were escaping from Egypt, the Israelites saw the Shekinah glory as light, but the Egyptians saw only darkness. God could have done something similar for the magi."

Wow! That was interesting. Rosie realized she needed to study her Bible more. She'd always thought the star was like one of the stars she saw in the sky on a clear night, only larger.

"When did the wise men see the baby Jesus?" Jamie asked.

"They probably didn't see Jesus as an infant," Jonathan answered. "The Bible uses a different word for Jesus when the magi arrived—

2 Matthew 2:9
3 Luke 2:9

paidion (young child) versus *brephos* (newborn). And by the time the wise men arrived, Mary and Joseph were in a house rather than a stable. Jesus might have been one or two years old by then."

"Why did they give Jesus gold, frankincense, and myrrh?" Jared asked. "Those seem like strange gifts for a child."

"They knew this wasn't just any child," Jonathan stated. "He was a very special child! Many believe the gifts were symbolic. Gold to show He was a king, frankincense because He was God, and myrrh to indicate He was the perfect man who would die for our sins."

"Jared, you should research the gifts more," Julie suggested. "It's interesting to learn what exactly they were and perhaps why they were given."

Jared nodded. "I'll do that."

"These wise men have given us a lot to think about," Grandma said. "Are there any more questions for them?"

When no one said anything, she continued, "I find it interesting that most of the Jewish people didn't notice the birth of their Savior, yet these Gentiles made a long journey seeking Christ so they could worship Him. The Bible says that if we seek Christ with all our hearts, we'll find Him."[4]

Rosie wondered about Abigail. Was she seeking anything? Maybe Jared had been right to invite her to be part of the nativity. Playing Mary might help her find God.

Jessie jumped off her father's lap. "Only three more weeks until the live nativity!"

"That's right," Grandma said. "Tomorrow is our first practice! We still have a lot of work to do to get ready."

Rosie frowned. She was going to miss all the fun.

---

4   Jeremiah 29:13

14

Nativity Practice

The Quarter Horse's eye was not quite right. Rosie erased it and tried to draw it again, but it didn't look any better the second time. She put her pencil down and closed the tablet. The house was so quiet she was having a hard time concentrating on drawing. She walked over and looked out the living room window. It was like looking through a time machine back to the days of Christ.

People were walking around in the costumes Grandma had made. Wooden backdrops that formed the buildings for the different scenes had been set up around the driveway loop between the barn and the house.

For the practices, they would use a doll for baby Jesus, but someone from their church was allowing them to use their infant on the night of the real performance. Rosie couldn't imagine any mother trusting her baby to Abigail's care, but it would make the scene realistic.

Rosie couldn't stand to stay in the house any longer. The stairs were still off-limits. Since she couldn't get her coat from her room, she found her mom's jacket hanging on a hook on the back porch. It came down to her knees, but she wrapped it around herself and walked back through the living room.

When she stepped out the front door, the cold, fresh air hit her face. It seemed like it had been years since she'd been outside. Even more than the nativity practice, she wanted to see the horses. She missed Scamper and couldn't wait until her ribs healed enough that she could ride again. She walked slowly toward the barn.

"What are you doing out here?"

Oh no! Her grandmother had spotted her. "Please, Grandma, I'm feeling better—really! I can't stand staying inside one more minute! Can I go see Scamper?"

Eric ran to her side and grabbed her arm. "Come on. I'll help you to the barn. After that, you need to sit down and rest."

Rosie smiled, relieved that they weren't going to make her go right back inside. When she stepped into the barn, she inhaled the scent of hay and horsehair—but she was careful not to breathe too deeply. When they reached Scamper's stall, her dad opened the door. Scamper stepped forward and nickered to her.

"Hello, boy. I've missed you so much! Have you missed me?" Rosie had never been away from him for so long before. She gave him a kiss on the nose and a good rub under his neck.

He nudged her for a treat. She reached into her pocket and pulled out a mint. "Of course, I didn't forget. Here you go. Now be a good boy." She patted him and continued down the aisle. "How are Charley and Rascal?"

Eric closed Scamper's door and caught up with her as she approached the ponies' stall.

When he opened the next door, Rosie only saw one pony. "Hello, buddy." She rubbed Charley's forehead, then turned to her dad. "Where's Rascal?"

Eric hesitated. "Rosie."

"Those two are best buddies. They're always together. Is Rascal out in the corral?"

Eric shook his head. "No, honey. We took Rascal back to the Amish farm."

"What?" Rosie was so shocked she didn't know whether to be angry or to cry. "Why, Dad? He didn't do anything wrong! It was my fault. I didn't know how to control him."

"We can't have a pony here that runs off. You know that. He might hurt one of the kids who come to our camps."

"But, Dad!" Rosie's eyes began to fill with tears. "The gunshots scared him. That guy wasn't supposed to be on our property."

"I understand that, but Rascal took off when he heard the shots—Charley didn't. We need horses and ponies like Charley that aren't easily frightened."

Rosie leaned against the stall and cried. "I spent so much time training him, and he was doing so well."

Eric put his arm around her. "Don't forget, I spent a lot of time with him too. He was my first training project. I'm almost as disappointed as you are. Grandma says some ponies make great cart ponies—and others don't."

Rosie didn't know what to say.

"Think about the kids we had at our camps this summer. Many of them had never been around horses before. What if Rascal had taken off with Annabelle in the cart?"

Rosie knew her dad was right. Annabelle would have been scared if Rascal had run off with her. But now she didn't have a pony to drive for the nativity.

"Rascal's a sweet boy. They'll find a good home for him with kids who have more experience. He just didn't work out for us here."

Rosie nodded and wiped her eyes.

"You want to go outside and watch the practice? They should be about ready to start."

"I guess so." Rosie took her dad's hand and walked out of the barn. She sat on the bench outside the door to watch. She wiped away her tears and tried not to think about Rascal.

"Everyone to their starting positions," Grandma called out.

Rosie had to smile when she saw Abigail sitting sidesaddle on the little donkey, Gus, with Billy leading her. Abigail didn't exactly appear to be "great with child." They'd have to stuff a pillow inside her costume the night of the performance.

Billy led the donkey toward the first scene, where Jared was the innkeeper. When they stopped in front of the inn, Jared shook his head and pointed to the next scene, the stable.

Billy yelled, "What do you mean you don't have any room?" He turned and yanked on the donkey's lead rope. Poor Gus made a sudden, sharp turn to his left.

"Oh no!" Rosie could see Abigail start to wobble, but Billy's back was to her.

Abigail clutched at the donkey's mane, but there wasn't enough of the sparse hair to hold onto. "Aagh!" She lost her balance and toppled backward off the donkey.

The last thing Rosie saw was Abigail's boots going over Gus' back. She tried not to laugh.

Billy must have heard the thud when Abigail hit the ground. He spun around. "Abigail! What happened?"

"What happened?" Abigail stood up and brushed dirt from her costume. "You're too stupid to know how to lead that smelly little donkey! That's what happened!" Abigail smacked Gus on the hindquarters.

The startled donkey jumped and trotted around Billy, hiding behind him for protection.

Abigail removed her costume, threw it onto the ground, and stomped off toward the barn.

"I'm sorry," Billy called after her. "I was just trying to make the scene more realistic."

Grandma motioned for everyone to continue with the practice. "Gus is so small I don't see how she could be hurt, but I'll go check on her."

Rosie had been so sad about Rascal, but now she couldn't stop smiling as she replayed in her mind the moment Abigail fell off the small donkey. She wondered if her grandmother could talk the girl into continuing to be Mary. What a crazy start to their nativity!

In the next scene, the shepherds were out in the fields with their flocks. There were shepherds of various sizes in the group. Since she couldn't be Mary, Jessie had reluctantly agreed to be a shepherd when her mom promised that she could be in charge of one of the real sheep.

After that was Herod's palace. The pastor of their church was King Herod. Eric, Robert, and Jonathan were the wise men on horseback, riding Scamper, Zach, and Scout.

When the practice ended, Jared and Billy walked over to Rosie.

"What was that all about, Billy?" she asked.

He grinned sheepishly. "I was trying to imagine how Joseph might have felt that night when Mary was about to have the baby, and no one had room for them. I guess I went a little overboard."

"No," Jared laughed, "Abigail's the one who went overboard."

"Very funny," Billy said. "Is she all right?"

Rosie shrugged. "I don't see how she could have gotten hurt. She's probably just embarrassed. The great trail rider falling off that little donkey!"

"I hope we don't have to find another Mary," Jared said.

"I'll be Mary!" Jessie yelled as she trotted past on Gus, waving one hand in the air. "See! I won't fall off!"

Jared stared at the little donkey. "Poor Gus."

Oh no. Not again. Jessie didn't really think she could be Mary now, did she? Rosie suddenly felt cold and tired. She shivered and hugged her mom's coat tighter to herself.

Eric walked over carrying a stack of costumes he had collected from the participants. "Where's Grandma? I don't know what she wants done with these."

119

"Can I go in now, Dad?"

Eric gave Rosie a funny look. "Are you all right?"

Rosie had surprised herself with the request to go inside. "I've been sitting around the house so long; I guess I'm out of shape."

Eric handed the costumes to Billy; then he helped Rosie back into the house.

Once inside, Rosie stretched out on the couch, opened her sketchpad, and thumbed through the pages. Three of the drawings were finished. She wasn't sure how many to do—maybe ten or twelve. She held a page up, stared at it, and smiled. These were the best horses she'd ever drawn. She couldn't wait to see the look on Abigail's face when she gave her the gift. She pulled out a pencil and went back to work on the eye of that Quarter Horse.

15

Christmas Eve

After falling off Gus at the first practice, Rosie never imagined Abigail would continue with her role as Mary. She was surprised when the girl returned for the second and third practices. To Rosie's relief, between the fall from the donkey and the fact that Billy ignored Abigail when they weren't practicing, the girl's crush on him seemed to be over.

Rosie's ribs felt almost back to normal. She hadn't run since the accident, but had worked up to a fast walk. She was still two weeks away from being fully cleared by her doctor for all activities, but he had somewhat reluctantly given his approval for driving the pony cart.

Rosie walked into the barn and found Carrie grooming Charley in his stall. "Is he ready?"

Carrie braided a bright red bow into the pony's forelock. "He's excited about tonight. Aren't you, Charley?"

The pony chewed a mouthful of hay and stared at them.

"He doesn't look too excited, but I can't wait!" Rosie checked her watch.

"How much longer?" Carrie snapped a rubber band around the bottom of the braid.

"About two hours."

The girls had agreed to take turns driving Charley. Rosie wished things had worked out with Rascal so they could have used both ponies, but at least she had recovered enough to drive Charley for part of the evening.

Rosie had envisioned snowflakes falling as they acted out the Christmas scenes, but it didn't look like that was going to happen either. They were still waiting for the first snowfall of the season.

The women were working in the barn lounge, getting it ready for serving refreshments. People from their church had donated eighty dozen homemade Christmas cookies. Rosie had never seen so many cookies in her life. Two enormous coffee pots on the counter would hold the hot chocolate, but the rest of the space was filled with stacks of cookie boxes. Forty gallon jugs of milk sat on the floor of the girls' bunkhouse in the barn. No ready-made powdered mix—Grandma insisted on using her own secret hot chocolate recipe for this special occasion.

That was enough refreshments to serve five hundred. Rosie couldn't imagine that many people coming to the nativity. She hoped they'd have dozens of cookies left over! They had sent out flyers and run ads in the local paper, but there was no way to tell how many people might show up.

At dusk, the first guests began to arrive, parking in the areas Billy and Jared had roped off on both sides of the drive.

Rosie hurried to join Carrie at the barn. "They're coming!"

Charley was tied to the hitching post, ready to go. They would take two or three children at a time in the cart. Everyone else would walk from scene to scene.

Carrie pointed to the pony. "You go first."

"Are you sure?" Rosie grinned. "You've worked with Charley more than I have. You should go first."

"No. I want you to."

Rosie didn't argue. "Thanks, Carrie!" She climbed into the cart, backed Charley up, and drove to the loading area where several parents and children were waiting.

Two young children were first in line. Rosie guessed the little girl with curly, blonde hair was about three. Her brother appeared to be a year or two older. Carrie helped them into the cart and showed them where to hold on.

"What's your name?" Rosie asked the girl.

"Lindsey."

"I'm Brett," the little boy said.

Lindsey pointed to the pony in front of them. "What's his name?"

"That's Charley."

"Can I pet him?" The girl stood up and leaned forward to touch the pony.

"No!" Rosie didn't want her first passenger to fall out of the cart. She grabbed Lindsey and gently pulled her back onto the seat. "Not yet. When we're finished, you can pet him. In a few minutes, Charley will take us around so we can see a story about the birth of Jesus."

Lindsey looked around. "Where is Jesus?"

"He hasn't been born yet," Brett said. "Has He, ma'am?"

Ma'am? Rosie smiled. She'd never been called that before. Did she look that old to these children? "Jesus was really born a long time ago," she tried to explain. "Some people are going to do a play to show us what it was like in Bible times."

"What time was He born?" Brett persisted.

"Oh no, I didn't mean that kind of time. No one knows the exact time he was born. We'll get started in a few minutes, and you'll see what I mean about acting out the story."

Brett and Lindsey turned and waved to their parents.

Rosie sat quietly watching the darkened left side of the barn where Billy waited for the signal from Grandma to begin his journey. When he walked out wearing a long brown robe leading Gus, Rosie motioned for the children to look in that direction.

Lindsey's eyes grew wide, and she clapped her hands as the donkey walked by them. "A real donkey!"

Abigail was convincing as Mary. She held her hand over her heavily padded stomach and winced with each step the little donkey took. Rosie hoped she wouldn't fall off again. She didn't want anything to ruin the Christmas story that night.

Rosie whispered, "That's Joseph and Mary." She clucked to Charley, and the pony walked toward the innkeeper scene.

Billy knocked at the door of the inn. "I need a room for my wife and myself."

Jared, the innkeeper, listened to Billy and then shook his head. "Sorry. I have no more room here!" He waved the couple away and closed the door.

Billy flung his hands up in the air and said something that Rosie couldn't hear. He was still adding to Joseph's part, but this time he carefully turned Gus around and continued walking.

"Why couldn't they stay there?" Brett wanted to know.

"The inn was full," Rosie said. "They didn't have room for Mary and Joseph."

Next was the manger scene. Rather than just a backdrop propped up from behind with two-by-fours, Billy and Eric had built this one more substantially. It was a small, three-sided shelter with a roof that would provide protection for Mary, Joseph, and the baby in case of bad weather. A curtain had been draped across the front, closing the inside off from the view of the guests.

Joseph tied the donkey to a post, helped Mary down, and led her around behind the scene. They would enter through a back door so Mary was out of sight when she lost her padding.

Lindsey looked all around. "Where did they go?"

Rosie held her finger to her lips. "Shh. You'll see."

In a few minutes, the curtain opened, revealing Mary and Joseph kneeling beside a wooden manger. A real baby lay on top of the hay. Mary stood and picked the infant up, cradling him in her arms. She adjusted the blankets around him and stared into the baby's face.

Lindsey pointed. "A baby!"

Brett nodded. "That's baby Jesus!"

Rosie whispered. "Remember, it's just a play, but you're right; they're showing us what it was like when Jesus was born." Charley moved forward until they were halfway between the manger scene and the following one so they could see both.

In the next scene, a spotlight focused on Lauren, the angel who appeared to the shepherds to announce the birth of Christ. The shepherds, including Jamie and Jessie, shook with fear. Then a multitude of the heavenly host appeared singing and praising God. About twenty children from their homeschool group had volunteered for that role.

The shepherds talked among themselves and then began their journey to find the baby who was wrapped in swaddling clothes and lying in a manger.

Rosie pointed out the small flock of sheep and goats to Lindsey and Brett. Jessie's sheep bleated as it followed her to the manger scene, where the shepherds knelt before the baby.

When Charley reached the following scene, three wise men rode up on horseback, their long, colorful robes trailing down over the horses' hindquarters.

Charley bobbed his head and whinnied to greet his friend Scamper. The visitors, gathered in front of the scene, turned to look at the small pony. Rosie pulled on his reins a little and whispered loudly, "No, Charley! You're not allowed to talk to Scamper right now."

After inquiring of King Herod where to find the newborn king of the Jews, the wise men rode on to find Jesus as an older child in a house. Other people played Mary, Joseph, and Jesus in that scene since Billy and Abigail were still at the manger.

The wise men dismounted and knelt before Jesus, presenting their gifts of gold, frankincense, and myrrh. Then they remounted the horses and cantered off.

Rosie held Charley still, watching until the wise men's horses disappeared into the darkness. "That's the end," she told the children.

"I wanna ride some more," whined Brett.

"I'll take you back to where we started," Rosie said, "but then you have to hop out so the next kids can have a turn."

She trotted Charley back to where the children's parents waited. "Climb out, and you can give Charley a quick pet."

Rosie stepped out of the cart after the children. Brett and Lindsey petted Charley's long, shaggy coat. The pony snorted and made them jump.

Brett backed away and started to climb into the cart again. "I want another ride!"

"Not tonight." Rosie shook her head. "But come back another time. We're going to start giving cart rides at the farm—and sleigh rides if it ever snows."

"But I want to ride tonight," Brett pouted.

Rosie knew how to solve that problem. "Do you like cookies?"

Brett perked up when he heard the word "cookies." He and his sister nodded.

"There's hot chocolate and cookies inside." Rosie pointed toward the open barn door. "Merry Christmas! I hope you enjoyed the nativity." She waved and watched the children walk with their parents into the barn.

Rosie held Charley's reins while Carrie stepped into the cart. "That was fun! The kids loved it."

The girls alternated turns with each group that went through the nativity. When Rosie wasn't driving Charley, she scooted into the barn for a hot chocolate. There were so many guests. She'd never dreamed that many people would come!

The cookies were rapidly disappearing. Rosie grabbed a couple of gingerbread men before they were all gone—one for her and one for Carrie. All the people talking at once created a buzz that was louder than the Christmas carols that played softly over the speakers in the barn. Abigail's parents were even there, and they seemed to be enjoying themselves. Rosie couldn't remember ever seeing Mr. Miller smile before.

After the last group finished the circuit, Rosie climbed into the cart beside Carrie, and they drove Charley around to each scene, letting the actors know that it was over.

"Abigail, you were great as Mary." Rosie noticed the girl now wore a pair of lined winter boots rather than the sandals she'd started the evening in. It wasn't as authentic—the boots looked a little funny with Mary's long dress, but they were much more practical.

"I'm glad we're finished. My toes are so cold I think they're about to fall off."

"At least you didn't fall off Gus this time," Billy laughed.

"That was your fault," Abigail reminded him. "You finally learned how to control the little beast."

Rosie nodded toward the barn. "There's hot chocolate inside. I saw your parents in there a while ago."

Abigail turned and walked toward the barn.

"This was a great idea, Rosie," Billy said. "At first when Eric said I should be in it, I didn't want to, but since it was your dad, I couldn't say no."

"Your second-grade teacher was wrong," Rosie said. "You're a great actor."

"Thanks." Billy seemed a little embarrassed by the compliment. "I loved being Joseph. It made the Christmas story seem more real to me."

"I wish Abigail's part would have had the same effect on her," Jared said, "but I don't think it did."

"I never imagined she'd even be in it," Rosie said. "The message might sink in after a while."

"Come on. I need some hot chocolate." Billy blew on his hands. "Joseph forgot to bring his gloves, so my fingers might be frostbitten."

"Hey, wait for me!" Jessie ran toward them. She'd already pulled her shepherd costume off, but her faithful sheep was still by her side.

"What are you—a sheep whisperer?" Billy laughed. "That sheep follows you everywhere now."

"Looks like your sheep's having a bad hair day," Jared said.

Jessie leaned down and tried to smooth out the sheep's wooly coat. "Don't make fun of Mittens. She gave some of her wool for the baby Jesus."

Rosie eyed her suspiciously. "What did you do to her?"

"Nothing! Why are you always accusing me of doing something wrong?" Jessie patted the sheep's head. "Come on, girl. Let's go get some cookies."

"Mittens?" Jared shook his head. "What kind of a name is that for a sheep? Don't you dare take her into the barn! There are too many people in there. Put Mittens back in her pen."

Jessie frowned. "First, no presents. Now, no sheep. I can't have any fun. Come on, girl. I'll take you back to your wooly friends."

"I hate to tell you this," Rosie called after her, "but it might be no cookies too! Last time I was inside, there were hardly any left."

Jessie stopped and turned around. She stomped and put her hands on her hips, glaring at them. "Thanks a lot!"

"Sorry!" Rosie said.

Jared sighed. "I'm not sure my sister gets the real meaning of Christmas either."

"Wasn't it incredible?" Rosie asked as her grandmother closed the door of the barn lounge after they'd finished cleaning up. "I can't believe how many people came!"

"It was a huge success," Grandma agreed. "I can definitely see this becoming an annual event."

"Building those scenes and putting them up was more fun than taking them down will be," Eric groaned.

"I'll help you with them whenever you're ready," Billy offered.

"They're not going anywhere," Kristy said. "Let's not worry about it until after Christmas."

Billy turned toward his apartment. "Good night, everyone."

"You're joining us for breakfast?" Grandma asked.

Billy smiled. "If it involves food, you know I'll be there. See you all in the morning."

The family walked out of the barn together.

Julie waved and steered the twins toward her car. "We'll be back around lunchtime, Mom. Get some rest tonight."

"Julie and I will bring the food," Lisa added. "Don't go to any trouble fixing anything. We want you to have a break tomorrow. That's our Christmas gift to you on this no-gifts Christmas!"

Grandma smiled. "Thank you!"

Rosie waved to everyone, then she and Carrie followed Grandma and their mom and dad to the house. It felt as if they had already celebrated Christmas, but tomorrow was actually Christmas Day.

"I hope you two aren't planning to get up too early in the morning," her grandmother said as she walked through the front door. "I'm beat."

"I'm sleeping in." Carrie yawned. "I'm tired."

"Me too!" Rosie followed Carrie up the stairs. "Good night, Carrie. Merry almost-Christmas!"

Carrie covered her mouth, trying to stop another yawn. "Good night. See you in the morning."

Rosie flicked the light switch on in her room. She could have kicked herself for not having the booklet ready to give to Abigail that night. What if she didn't come to the stable tomorrow? It wouldn't be as special if she didn't give it to her on Christmas Day.

Rosie pulled the horse sketches out of her desk drawer. She selected a bright blue piece of construction paper and glued the drawing of Raja in the middle of it to use for the front cover. The remaining ten drawings were arranged in the order she wanted, with another blue sheet at the back. Then she stapled all the pages together.

She tapped her pencil on the desk, admiring her work. On the back of the book, she wrote, "Merry Christmas, Abigail! I know how much you love horses so I made these drawings for you. Love, Rosie."

She left the booklet on her desk and crawled into bed.

16

Christmas Morning

Despite promising to sleep in, Rosie was so excited about Christmas she was awake early the next morning. After dressing, she glanced out her bedroom window. Mr. Miller's truck was parked in front of the barn. Suddenly unsure about the gift, Rosie hoped Abigail hadn't come with him. That way she could hand the gift to Mr. Miller, and he could give it to her later.

Rosie picked up the book from her desk and grabbed a coat. She peeked into Carrie's room across the hall. Her sister was still asleep. It would have been nice to take her along, but there wasn't time to wake her. Since it was Christmas, Mr. Miller might not stay at the barn long. She crept down the stairs alone. Someone was rattling around in the kitchen. It was probably her grandmother. She was usually the first one up in the morning. Rosie tiptoed to the front door and slipped out.

As she approached the barn, she noticed that both of Abigail's parents were sitting in the truck. Rosie gulped and gave a quick wave. That meant Abigail must be in the barn. She'd have to give her the gift personally. She found the girl standing outside Raja's stall. Rosie held the book behind her back and walked toward her.

"Hey. Merry Christmas," Abigail greeted her rather flatly.

"Merry Christmas to you too!" Rosie still wasn't sure about the gift. Maybe it hadn't been such a great idea after all. "You didn't have to come out here to feed your horse on Christmas morning. We could do that."

"He's not my horse anymore," Abigail said abruptly. "My dad sold him."

"What?" Rosie was stunned.

"He's leaving today. I came to tell him good-bye."

Had Abigail known about this before? Rosie had seen her often over the past few weeks at the nativity practices, but the girl had never mentioned selling Raja. Her voice sounded different, but she didn't look sad. Still—she must care about the horse since she had come to see him one last time. Rosie couldn't imagine selling Scamper. That would be like losing a member of her family.

Maybe Abigail's dad was going to buy her that expensive horse she'd bragged about. Rosie felt awkward holding the gift behind her, but she didn't know what else to do with it. "Are you getting another horse?"

"I don't know." Abigail shrugged. "I might not ride anymore. I'm going to concentrate on playing tennis tournaments for a while."

Tennis? Rosie had no idea that Abigail played tennis. She realized that she didn't know her very well at all.

Oh, great. I made a book of horse pictures for a girl who doesn't have a horse anymore and may never ride again. Rosie would have taken the book back to the house, but at their next Bible study, everyone was supposed to talk about their experience with the gifts. She had to go through with it. She pulled the book out and extended it toward Abigail.

The girl took it from her. "What's this?"

"A Christmas gift. I thought you'd like the horse pictures."

Abigail stood there, not saying anything.

"I drew them," Rosie added.

Abigail looked at the booklet. "Why did you give me a gift? You don't even like me."

Rosie flinched. Was it that obvious? "That's Raja." She pointed to the sketch on the cover. "Open it. I added one of my favorite Bible verses to each page."

Abigail turned to the first page and read the verse, "I can do all things through Christ who strengthens me. Philippians 4:13." NKJV

The girl's face seemed rather expressionless. Rosie couldn't tell whether she liked the gift or not.

Abigail thumbed quickly through the rest of the book, then stared at Rosie. "Ah, I get it. You're trying to turn me into a Jesus freak like you and Billy and Jared, right? No one around here likes me. I can tell. I'm just a project for all of you."

Rosie took a quick breath. There was a little too much truth in what Abigail had said. She decided to explain the whole thing. "A few months ago, at our Bible study, we decided not to get any Christmas presents this year—"

"What? We're going to my grandparents when we leave here. My grandfather has even more money than my dad does. They always buy me the most awesome gifts."

Rosie half-listened, then continued with her explanation. "We agreed that gifts take our minds away from the real meaning of Christmas."

Abigail looked confused. "How can you have Christmas without gifts? Haven't you been to the mall in the last month? Everyone buys gifts for people at Christmas."

"I've never been to the mall."

"Oh, brother." Abigail rolled her eyes. "So Christmas is not about gifts, but…" She held up the book. "You're giving me a gift? That doesn't make sense."

Rosie was beginning to feel a little confused herself. "We decided we wouldn't *get* gifts, but each of us picked one person to *give* a gift to."

Abigail stared at her. "You picked me?" The girl's face softened, and she almost smiled.

Rosie *had* picked her, but of course, it hadn't been by choice. She felt a twinge of guilt. Not wanting to lie about it, she avoided answering the question. "I thought you'd like the horse pictures."

"Um, yeah. Thanks."

The conversation was becoming so awkward that Rosie wanted to turn around and run, but her ribs were still too sore for that. "Merry Christmas, Abigail." She stepped backward as she spoke so she wasn't turning her back on the girl. "I should go inside. Everyone must be awake by now."

"What do you do on a no-gifts Christmas?"

"I don't know." Rosie smiled. "We've never had one before."

"I guess I won't see you anymore, unless I get another horse— maybe when I can compete in the trail ride again."

Rosie wasn't sure what to say to that. She just wanted to end the conversation. "Okay. Bye."

She hurried to the other side of the barn to give Scamper a treat and to wish him a merry Christmas before going inside.

When Rosie opened the front door, she was immediately hit with the aroma of homemade cinnamon rolls and coffee. Coffee didn't appeal to her yet, but the smell of the rolls made her mouth water.

She washed up and then joined the others at the breakfast table.

"I thought you were going to sleep in this morning," Grandma said.

"I had to give Scamper a candy cane. He loves those things." Rosie didn't want to say anything about Abigail's book until later when the others gave their gifts.

"What about Zach and Charley?" Carrie asked. "Did you give them a treat too?"

"And Sassy?" Billy asked.

"No." Rosie watched her grandmother ice the last of the rolls. "Just my horse, because he's special!"

"Humph!" Billy said. "You don't want to get on my mule's bad side."

"When is everyone getting here?" Carrie asked.

Kristy sat down at the table beside her. "They should be here by lunchtime."

"Good," Rosie said. "What are we having?" She hadn't even eaten breakfast yet, but she was already thinking about lunch.

"Ostrich burgers and wild boar steaks," Billy teased.

Rosie rolled her eyes at him. "Maybe you are, but I'm not."

Grandma set the large plate of cinnamon rolls on the table, and Kristy poured milk in the girls' glasses. Eric prayed, and they all began to eat.

Her grandmother made the best cinnamon rolls. They'd had them on Christmas morning ever since Rosie could remember. She took a big bite of one. The sweet icing covered her lips, and she slowly licked it off, savoring the taste. "Mm. These are so good!"

"Don't talk with your mouth full," Kristy reminded her.

Rosie nodded and finished chewing. "What are we doing today, since we're not opening gifts?"

"I'm sure we'll find something to do." Grandma poured herself a cup of coffee. "Boredom has never been a problem when this family gets together."

"Billy, after breakfast I can give Sassy a treat if you want," Rosie offered. "I would have given all the horses one, but I only had one candy cane in my pocket."

Billy turned quickly toward Eric. "Uh, no, never mind. That mule is on a strict diet." He looked back at Rosie. "She needs to trim down if she's going to be in the mounted rescue group."

"O—kay." Billy's response seemed a little odd. He hadn't mentioned Sassy being on a diet, and she didn't see how one candy cane could make a difference anyway.

Rosie wasn't worried about her own diet—she managed to eat two of the huge rolls. She pushed her chair away from the table and slumped back, patting her stomach. "I'm stuffed!"

"Better not eat too much," Eric said. "If your stomach stretches any more, you may injure your ribs again."

"Funny, Dad."

"How about a game while we wait for the others to arrive?" Kristy suggested. "Horseopoly?"

Carrie ran upstairs and returned in a few minutes with the game. "Who wants to play?"

"Watch out," Grandma warned. "Carrie's an expert at that game."

Everyone joined in except Eric. Rosie was shuffling the game cards when she noticed her dad put on his jacket and go out the back door. He must be going to check on the animals they had borrowed for the nativity.

They were a couple hours into the board game, with Carrie winning, when Rosie heard the front door open. She hurried to the living room. Aunt Julie and her family had arrived.

Julie and Jonathan came through the door, each carrying a covered dish. Following them was a woman Rosie didn't recognize.

"This is our neighbor, Grace Wilson." Julie introduced her and then walked toward the kitchen.

"Merry Christmas, Grace. Here, let me take your coat," Grandma said. "I'm so glad you could join us."

Grandma had a way of making everyone feel welcome. Rosie remembered that name. Mrs. Wilson had to be the woman in the Operation Christmas Spirit gift drawing.

Jared walked over to Rosie, Carrie, and Billy and whispered, "When are we going to give our gifts?"

Rosie smiled. "I already did."

"What?" Carrie said. "Why didn't you tell me?"

"I'll explain later."

They agreed that the others would give their gifts after lunch. Rosie couldn't wait to see what gifts the others had come up with. She wondered if Abigail had shown the book of drawings to her parents. She hoped the verses on each page would encourage her to read the Bible—if Abigail even had a Bible.

17
The Gifts

Normally I read the Christmas story from Luke on Christmas Day," Eric said, "but after last night and all the practices, most of us have the story practically memorized."

Lisa and her family had arrived, along with Billy's dad, and they were all gathered in the big kitchen of the farmhouse. Rosie agreed with her father. After the Bible studies and the live nativity, she knew the Christmas story better than she ever had.

"Since we're not exchanging gifts this year, everyone could tell about a favorite Christmas gift they received in the past," Lisa suggested.

"That's a good idea," Kristy said. "Let's eat, and we can go around the table like we do at Thanksgiving."

Grandma steered Mrs. Wilson to the end of the table. Mr. King stood and pulled out the chair next to him, helping Mrs. Wilson to her seat.

The table was so full of all types of food there was barely room for everyone's plates. Eric prayed, then started a plate heaped with oven-roasted turkey around the table.

"Grandma, why don't you tell us your favorite gift first?" Rosie said.

"Hmm. Let me think about that."

Rosie piled mashed potatoes onto her plate and waited for her grandmother's answer.

Grandma didn't keep them waiting long. She set her coffee cup down and began, "When I was a little girl, we didn't have much money, but I didn't know it at the time. It wasn't until I was older that I realized how poor my family had been. Mainly what I remember about Christmas was how everyone gathered at my grandmother's house—much as we're doing right now. But my favorite Christmas gift when I was a girl was an art set one of my aunts gave me."

Rosie stopped chewing, and despite her mother's many warnings, spoke with food in her mouth. "You used to draw?" She'd never heard her grandmother say anything about that before.

Grandma nodded. "The set had a book with drawing lessons, several types of pencils, an eraser, and a sketch pad. I worked my way through all the lessons. As I completed each drawing, I taped my masterpiece up on the wall of the room I shared with my sisters. It was quite the art gallery when I was finished."

"But you don't draw now, Grandma." Rosie was still amazed that her grandmother shared her interest in drawing.

"It's been many years since I've drawn anything. When you get older and start working or raising a family, there's not always time to do everything."

"I'm never going to stop drawing," Rosie said.

"I hope you don't. You have more talent than I did."

"Thanks, Grandma."

Billy was next. "Pass."

Rosie looked at him. It sounded as if he were passing in a card game. "You can't think of any gifts—or you don't want to tell us?"

"I don't remember anything I got for Christmas."

Mr. King seemed a little hurt by his son's statement. "You're making me sound like a terrible parent, Billy. Don't you remember the wooden chessboard I made for you one year? You must have been about twelve. I bought a nice set of playing pieces for it too, but you weren't interested in learning the game. It must still be at the house somewhere."

"Oh, yeah. I do remember that." Billy smiled. "That was during my video game phase. Chess sounded too boring at the time. Maybe I'll go home and look for it."

"If you find it, bring it here," Jared said. "I'll play you. I love chess."

Kristy spoke next. "I remember one year Mom told us we were getting three presents each."

"Oh, yes," Grandma said. "I experimented with several things over the years to try to keep the focus on Christ rather than on gifts. My ideas never seemed to work too well, though."

"I remember that," Lisa said. "The gifts were to represent the letters of the word *joy*. The first gift was J for Jesus—something to help us grow spiritually. O was for Others—something we could use for other people. I think we received stationery so we could write letters. And the last was Y for Yourself—something fun for us."

Julie shook her head. "I don't remember J-O-Y."

"You must have been about four then," Grandma said, "too young to remember it."

"What I remember most about Christmas is the church plays we were in every year," Julie said.

"We got the best parts because Mom was always the director," Lisa laughed.

"You got the best parts because you were the best actresses," Grandma insisted. "I'll have to look for the recordings of those plays. I bet the kids would like to see them."

143

After they had gone all the way around the table, Jared stood up and tapped his spoon on the side of his glass It sounded as if he were about to make an official proclamation.

"You all know we decided not to receive any gifts this Christmas, but the part of Operation Christmas Spirit you don't know about was that we each picked someone to give a gift to. None of us knows whose name the others have. We agreed to keep it a secret until today."

Rosie was certain she knew who everyone else had, but she couldn't wait to see what the gifts were.

Jared pulled an envelope out of his back pocket, then he walked over and handed it to Mrs. Wilson.

"For me?" She stared at the envelope. "But I didn't bring a gift for anyone."

Jared smiled. "That's the whole idea. We wanted to give a gift without expecting anything in return. Sorry. It got a little wrinkled in my pocket."

Mrs. Wilson opened the envelope and pulled out a piece of paper. "A coupon?"

Jared nodded. "For yard work. I'll mow your yard and weed your flowers once a week next summer."

"Oh, my! You can't do that for free," Mrs. Wilson said. "How much should I pay you?"

"Nothing. It's a gift," Jared insisted. "Your yard isn't big. It won't take me long."

Jared had Mrs. Wilson? Rosie was surprised. She'd thought Jessie had that name.

"My husband, Richard, always kept the yard and flowers so beautiful," Mrs. Wilson said. "I'm afraid I've neglected them."

"I can fix that," Jared said.

"Thank you, Jared. This is such a wonderful surprise. I wasn't expecting a gift at all. I wonder—are you any good at fixing cars? My old Betsy has developed a peculiar rattle."

Jared laughed. "Sorry. I can't help you there. The only engines I know anything about are the one-horsepower ones with four hooves and a tail."

Billy's dad cleared his throat. "I can take a look at that car for you, ma'am."

"Oh, could you? That would be wonderful. And call me Grace, please."

"All right, Grace, if you'll call me Daniel." He smiled. "We'll work out a time later. I don't want to interrupt what the kids are doing here."

Jared pointed to Jamie, who stood up next.

"I have Annabelle's name." Jamie still had the small slip of crumpled paper that Rosie had written the name on, and she held it up. "Annabelle was a girl at our camp this summer. I don't have anything for her yet, except an idea. What I was thinking was that we could let her come to camp again next summer for free." Jamie glanced around the table. "I mean, if it's all right with everyone."

"That's a great idea, Jamie," Kristy said. "A camp scholarship. We could do that for a different child every year."

"Sounds good to me," Grandma agreed. "And who better for the first recipient than Annabelle!"

Jamie smiled. "Great! If you can find her address, I'll write a letter to tell her about it." She pointed to Rosie and sat down.

Rosie had figured Jamie had Kristy's name. Wrong again. Obviously, she had no idea whose name anyone had.

"I don't have anything to show either. Abigail was my person. I made her a book of horse drawings and added one of my favorite Bible verses to each page."

"So that's what you were doing when you were recovering from the accident," Carrie said. "I knew you were drawing more than usual, but I thought it was because you didn't have anything else to do."

Rosie smiled. "It was fun working on it right beside you, knowing that you had no idea it was for Abigail."

"Where's the book?" Grandma asked. "I'd love to see it."

Rosie wished she could have shown it to her family. "I gave it to Abigail this morning."

"That explains what you were doing at the barn so early," Grandma said.

Rosie nodded.

"Did she like it?" Kristy asked.

"I think so, but I'm not sure. It was hard to tell." Rosie turned to her grandmother. "Did you know they sold Raja?"

"What? No one said anything to me about it. You'd think since their horse is boarded here, they would have let me know," Grandma muttered.

"The new owners are picking him up today. Abigail was here to say goodbye to him. She told me she might give up riding to play tennis."

"Who would give up riding for tennis?" Billy said. "That's ridiculous."

"I agree!" Rosie smiled and pointed at him to go next.

"My turn?" Billy held up one finger. "Hold on. I'll be back in a minute!" He got up and trotted out the back door.

"You kids are amazing me," Grandma said. "What a great idea your Operation Christmas Spirit is! And you've put so much thought into these gifts."

Soon there was a tapping at the back door, and Jared ran to open it. He and Billy struggled to get a large object, covered in a plain white sheet, through the door. Leave it to Billy to come up with such fancy wrapping.

Billy scooted the gift over in front of Kristy. "Merry Christmas!"

"This is for me? But I didn't expect anything."

"That's the point." Billy stood back and watched. "Go ahead. Open it!"

Kristy pulled the sheet off to reveal an end table made from a solid slab of wood. "Oh, Billy!" She ran her hand over the smooth finish. "It's beautiful."

"I made it." Billy grinned.

"What?" Kristy's eyes widened. "How could you make something like this?"

"Well, actually, God did most of the work. It's from a big old maple branch I found in the woods."

Rosie walked over to get a closer look at the table. "That's from the log Sassy was pulling that day Carrie and I saw you?"

"Yeah. You weren't supposed to be around when I brought it up to the barn."

"You said it was for your dad," Rosie reminded him.

"It was—kind of," Billy's dad said. "I have what's left of the log in my workshop at home. I could make more chessboards or—" he nodded toward Mrs. Wilson, "some flower pots."

"There's still plenty of wood left," Billy said. "I took it to a sawmill, and they cut that slab out for me. Then all I had to do was sand and varnish it and attach the metal legs."

"Billy, if you hadn't decided to be a paramedic, I'd say you could start your own furniture business making tables like this," Eric said.

147

"Thanks." Billy smiled. "Dad taught me a lot about working with wood."

"Maybe you could make one for me too," Grandma suggested.

"I will—if I have enough time." Billy sat back down at the kitchen table. "How about Carrie next?"

Carrie ran out of the kitchen and returned in a few minutes carrying a three-ring binder. She stood at the head of the table. "I have Grandma's name."

Grandma looked surprised. "Me?"

Carrie smiled and nodded. "One of my first memories of you was when you told me the story about Kezzie's birth. I love all the stories you tell about horses, so I decided to write them down."

She handed the notebook to her grandmother. "When you have time to read these, you can let me know if I got anything wrong. I have all of it saved on the computer so I can make changes easily."

Grandma took the notebook and carefully opened it. "Oh, Carrie, you don't know how much this means to me. I've told these stories for years, but I've never taken the time to put them into writing. Thank you so much!"

"You're welcome." Carrie sat back down. "Now that it's not a secret anymore, Rosie can draw some illustrations, and we can put it all together into a real book."

"Sure. I can do that." Rosie felt a little disappointed. She wished Abigail had been as excited about her gift as everyone else seemed to be.

It was Lauren's turn next. She handed a card to the person beside her. "Pass that down to Mr. King, please."

Rosie took a closer look at it before passing it on. The card was an invitation with fancy gold engraving around the edges.

When it reached Billy's dad, he read the invitation aloud, "You are cordially invited to join us for a family meal at Sonrise Stable on the last Sunday of every month at 6 p.m."

Billy leaned toward Rosie and whispered, "I think Dad would like it if Mrs. Grace Wilson was included in that invitation."

"What?" Rosie glanced toward the end of the table. Mrs. Wilson was watching Mr. King and smiling.

"Thank you, young lady," Daniel said. "You couldn't have given me a better gift. It's way too quiet at my house."

Billy laughed. "You never said that when I was at home."

"Son, I guess sometimes we don't appreciate what we have until we don't have it anymore."

"Yes, indeed," Mrs. Wilson agreed.

"I can guarantee it won't be quiet here," Grandma said. "Lauren, do you mind if we extend that invitation to include Mrs. Wilson?"

Apparently, her grandmother had also sensed something about Billy's dad and Mrs. Wilson. Rosie looked at Billy, and he gave her a quick wink.

"It's fine with me," Lauren said. "I want to help make the meals so I can learn how to cook better."

"Oh my." Mrs. Wilson dabbed at the corner of her eye with her napkin. "Thank you. You're all so kind."

Jessie was the only one who hadn't given her gift. Rosie remembered how focused her cousin had been on presents for herself. That was how they had come up with the idea for Operation Christmas Spirit in the first place. She ran through the names in her head. Who hadn't received a gift yet?

Billy!

Jessie had Billy's name. Rosie couldn't imagine what she had gotten for him.

18

Jessie's Turn

~

"It's finally my turn! Did you guys make me go last on purpose?" Jessie jumped up. "Wait a minute!" She ran out of the room and returned carrying a large cardboard box.

Rosie stared at the box and tried to imagine what Billy's gift might be.

Jessie set the box on the kitchen floor and pulled out a plastic gift bag, but rather than giving it to Billy, she handed it to Grandma. Then she continued, pulling more bags from the box and giving one to each person at the table. When she'd gone all the way around, she stood back and smiled. "Open them!"

Rosie couldn't have been more surprised. Jessie had made presents for everyone? She opened hers and pulled out a wooden manger made from popsicle sticks. Inside the manger was a bit of hay. A clothespin baby Jesus, wrapped in a small strip of cloth, lay on top of the hay. She picked up the baby and examined it. Jessie had painted a face and hair on the head of the clothespin. The cloth was cut from a baby blanket. Under the baby's head was a round piece of wool—a small pillow for Jesus to lie on.

"These are great, Jessie. I'm sure baby Jesus would have loved the pillow," Rosie said. "Where'd you get the wool?"

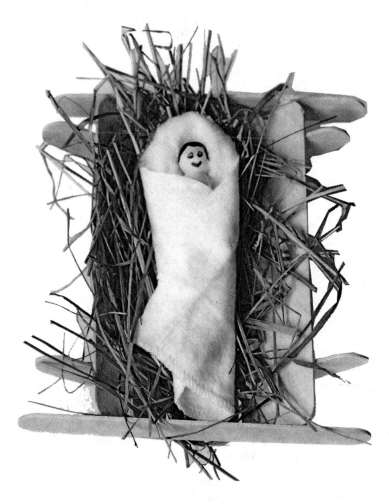

Jessie snuck a glance at her mom. "I—Uh, I better not say."

"What is that supposed to mean?" Julie looked sideways at her. "Where *did* you get the wool?"

"Well…" Jessie began slowly. "It's from Mittens, the sheep I had when I was a shepherd in the nativity."

"Oh, dear." Julie clapped her palm to her forehead.

"I snipped a little here and there. I told her it was for the baby Jesus, and she was okay with it. Really!"

"I cut off a little more than I needed though." Jessie reached into her box and held up a gallon Ziploc bag stuffed full of wool. "I don't know what to do with the rest of this!"

Jared laughed. "Poor Mittens! Does that sheep have any hair left? She must be freezing out there!"

"Why don't you learn to knit, Jessie? You could make some mittens—or a sweater for that poor bald sheep," Billy laughed.

Julie shook her head and tousled Jessie's hair. "What am I going to do with you?"

"Don't worry about their teasing," Grandma turned her manger around, examining it. "That was very kind of you to think of everyone at Christmas. And tell Mittens thank you for us too!"

Jessie squeezed her bag of wool and smiled.

Rosie stared at the manger in front of her. She still couldn't believe Jessie had made one of these for everyone. It must have taken her a long time. "What happened to the girl who was making up a Christmas list in October?"

Jessie smiled. "At first I *was* only thinking of myself, but then I realized how selfish that was. After that, I pretended to still be selfish just to trick everyone."

"It worked," Rosie laughed. "You were beginning to annoy me."

"Wait a minute," Billy said. "I thought everyone had already received their gifts. Whose name does Jessie have then?"

Rosie smiled. "The mystery person."

"Oh, yeah," Billy said. "I forgot we added someone else's name. Are you going to tell us who it is, Jessie? Or are you just going to stand there all day?"

She wiggled her index finger and smiled. "Everyone has to come outside." Jessie was so excited that she ran out the front door without her coat.

That was odd. What kind of gift was it, that Jessie couldn't bring it inside? Rosie hurried out the door without a coat too.

Jessie ran to the side of the barn where a black pickup sat parked next to Billy's rusty red one. "Merry Christmas, Billy!"

"What?" He stood in front of the truck as if frozen, his mouth hanging open. "I'm the mystery person?"

Jessie nodded. "How do you like your new truck?"

Rosie stared at her. If this was one of Jessie's jokes, it wasn't very funny.

Jonathan stepped up beside Jessie and patted the truck. "It belonged to a friend of mine—the absentminded professor type. He forgot to put oil in it and blew the engine; then he practically gave it to me. When Jessie asked me for help with her project, it seemed God had given us the perfect answer with this truck. It's yours, Billy."

Jessie climbed into the truck bed, beaming. "Dad and I went to three junkyards searching for an engine."

"When we found one, Eric and Robert helped me put it in," Jonathan said. "It purrs like a kitten now."

"You can't be serious." Billy looked dazed as he walked up to the truck and ran his hand along the side panels. "I've never had a truck that didn't have rust all over it."

"Your old one doesn't have rust, Billy," Rosie laughed. "It has holes where the rust used to be."

Jonathan held out a key. "A paramedic-in-training needs something reliable to drive back and forth to school."

Jessie jumped down from the truck. "What are you waiting for? Get in and try it out!"

Billy climbed in, and his dad hurried to the passenger side.

Everyone stepped back as Billy started the truck. Rosie could see him smiling through the window as he revved the engine. He pulled forward and drove around the driveway loop a few times.

Rosie was happy for Billy, but she was freezing. Her dad, who had thought to put a coat on, unbuttoned it and pulled Rosie into its warmth.

Billy parked the truck back where it had been and joined the group again. "I don't even..." his voice cracked, and he wiped tears from his eyes, "know what to say."

His dad patted him on the shoulder and then pulled him into a hug. "Just say thank you, son."

"Yeah." Billy stood next to his father with his arm around him. "Thank you, Jessie—and Jonathan, everyone! I don't know how I can repay you guys."

"You can't!" Jessie piped up. "That's the point. Remember?" She grinned from ear to ear, overjoyed about the gift she'd given Billy.

"Hey, Billy." Jared walked over and stood beside him. "Can I have your old truck?"

Billy fished a key out of his pocket and handed it to him. "She's all yours! Better pray she doesn't fall apart before you're old enough to drive her."

Jared took the key and ran to sit in his rusty new truck while everyone else oohed and aahed over Billy's. Then they hurried back into the house and jostled for a spot in front of the fireplace—all except Grandma, who went to the kitchen to make a big pot of hot chocolate.

19
God's Gift

A fter a dinner of leftovers and far too many desserts,
everyone watched *A Christmas Carol* together. When the
movie ended, Mr. King stood and announced that he had to return
to work the next day, so he would have to leave. Mrs. Wilson and
Billy walked out with him. Julie and Lisa's families packed up their
things and soon left too.

Rosie plopped into the recliner she had spent so much time
in while recovering from the accident, wondering why Christmas
couldn't go on forever. She'd never imagined that a Christmas
without receiving gifts could have turned out so well.

"Carrie, can you give me your notebook with—" Rosie stopped
when she realized her sister wasn't in the room. Carrie must have
gone upstairs. In fact, it seemed that everyone had vanished, except
her father.

"Do you want to help me feed the horses?"

"Sure, Dad." Rosie put on her heavy coat and walked beside
her father to the barn. She'd feed Charley first so she could spend
more time with Scamper. She reminded herself not to toss the hay
over the stall door. She pushed a flake into the pony's rack. Her ribs

were almost fully healed, and she didn't want to take the chance of reinjuring them.

She gave Charley a small candy cane and watched as he crunched it. Rosie thought about Rascal. Maybe the pony had been a Christmas gift for some boy or girl who would love and take care of him. She stared at Raja's empty stall. She still couldn't believe Abigail's father had sold the horse.

Rosie walked over to the stacked hay and cut the twines on another bale. Scamper needed an extra helping for his Christmas dinner. She wound the twines together and walked to the trash barrel to throw them away. It hadn't been emptied after last night's event, and the trash was overflowing. When she pushed it down to make more room, a flash of blue caught her eye. The twines fell from her hand, and she leaned forward for a closer look.

"What?" Rosie reached into the barrel and tugged on a bright blue piece of paper. Out from under a pile of cups and paper plates came the book she had made for Abigail. Her eyes burned as she stared at it. She pressed the book up against the wall and tried to smooth the crumpled pages with the palm of her hand, but the wrinkles remained. Rosie noticed a hot chocolate stain across the back cover.

She slumped against the wall and slid slowly down to the floor. The booklet fell from her hands and dropped onto the ground beside her. She put both hands on her head and began to sob.

"Are you all right, honey?" Eric came running. "What's wrong? Did you hurt your ribs again?"

Rosie shook her head, picked up the booklet, and handed the wrinkled pages to her dad. She wiped her eyes on her coat sleeve.

Eric sat down beside her and paged through the book. "You drew these? Rosie, they're very good."

"It's the book I made for Abigail." Rosie sniffed and searched her pockets for a tissue. "Dad, I worked so hard on that book, for weeks—and she threw it in the trash."

Eric turned to the first page and went through the book again, this time reading each verse aloud.

When he finished, he set the book on his lap, and they sat in silence for a few minutes. Rosie stared at the sketch of Raja on the cover.

"At first I was mad that I picked her name. I couldn't think of a single thing to give her. Then, when I had to rest for so long after the accident, I got the idea to make the book. I was so excited about it."

Rosie started crying again. "Dad, I really thought she would like it."

"Oh, sweetheart." Eric put an arm around his daughter and wiped his eyes with his other hand. "I have no idea why she threw this away. I can see the work and the love you put into every page. These are some of the best drawings you've ever done."

Rosie looked up at him. "You mean it?"

"Absolutely! Do you mind if I keep it?"

"Oh, Dad. It's all wrinkly—and it has hot chocolate on it."

Eric picked the book up again and sniffed the page with the stain on it. "A scented horse book. What a great idea!"

Rosie smiled through her tears.

"I'll set some heavy books on it, or I could borrow Grandma's iron and try to press the wrinkles out."

Rosie leaned against her father's side and felt his strong arm tighten around her. She had thought it before, but at that moment she was certain she had the best dad in the whole world.

"We'll have to pray for Abigail. Something must be wrong in her life that she couldn't appreciate the love that went into your gift."

Rosie blew her nose and nodded.

"You know, it's similar to what people do to God."

She tilted her head up toward her father. "What do you mean?"

"When people reject Jesus, it's like taking God's precious gift and tossing it in the trash."

Rosie thought about the pain she had felt in her heart upon discovering the book in the trash. In a way, it had hurt more than her broken ribs. Was that how God felt when people rejected Him?

"Dad, I hope I don't see Abigail again."

"I understand why you feel that way." He stroked her hair. "Since they sold Raja, she might not come back. But if she does, I'll help you talk to her."

"Thanks, Dad."

Eric stood. "Come on. Let's check on Sassy. Do you have an extra candy cane for her?"

Rosie patted the pocket of her jeans. She smiled when her dad tucked the book carefully under his arm.

They walked across the arena to the other side of the barn. When Rosie closed the gate behind her and turned toward the aisle, she saw a huge red bow hanging on the front of the stall next to Sassy's.

"What's that?" She hurried to the stall and started to slide the door open.

"SURPRISE!"

Rosie jumped and let out a little shriek when Grandma, her mom, Billy, and the rest of the family sprang up from their hiding places in the surrounding stalls. They hadn't gone home after all. What was going on?

A high-pitched whinny sounded from inside the stall.

Her heart thumped. Was Rascal back? She hurried into the stall, then stopped and stared. A buckskin pony stared back at her.

"What?" Rosie sputtered. "Who is this?"

Eric leaned against the open door. "Your new driving pony."

"You're kidding!"

"We were all sad about what happened with Rascal," Julie explained, "so we began searching for another pony for you to drive."

"For me?" Rosie ran her hand down the pony's neck.

"She belongs to all of us, but you can be the first one to drive her," Grandma said.

"I wanted to find a miniature mule for you," Billy said. "You know—Sassy the Super Mule in a pint-sized version, but those are hard to come by."

Rosie smiled. She'd never heard of a miniature mule. She held her hand out to the pony. "What's her name?"

"Treasure," Carrie said.

"We hoped to find a pony in time for the nativity, but it was more difficult to locate a good one than we anticipated," Kristy said. "We found Treasure just a couple days ago, which didn't leave enough time for you to practice driving her."

"She's already trained," Grandma added. "She's been driven in parades, shows, fairs, everything. Steady as a rock. We didn't want to take the chance of having another accident."

Treasure sniffed Rosie's hand.

"You're beautiful!" Rosie rubbed the pony's forehead, then looked at Carrie. "You knew about this?"

Carrie smiled. "Yes."

Jessie nodded vigorously. "Everyone knew about it but you."

"I can't believe you could keep this a secret, Jessie," Rosie said.

"She couldn't," Jared laughed. "That's why we didn't tell her until a few minutes ago when we all came out to the barn."

"But I still knew before Rosie," Jessie insisted. "And I can too, keep a secret. I kept Billy's truck a secret, didn't I?"

Rosie leaned against the stall wall and watched Treasure eat her hay. The pony was amazingly calm for having moved to a new home that day. She realized this must have been what her dad was doing when she saw him slip out of the house after breakfast.

161

Sassy pressed her big head against the divider between the two stalls, trying to get a better view of her new neighbor.

"I suppose this is what Sassy's sudden new diet plan was all about?" Rosie said.

Billy grinned. "Hey, I had to come up with something fast. Who would have thought you'd want to go visit Sassy on Christmas morning?"

Rosie glanced at the mule again. "You know what? Maybe that diet isn't such a bad idea after all!"

Billy covered Sassy's ears with his hands. "Shh! You'll hurt her feelings—and on Christmas Day! That's not nice."

"But it's the truth!" Jessie laughed.

Rosie would have liked to stay at the barn longer, getting acquainted with Treasure, but it was already late. She gave the pony a hug. "Good night, girl. I'll be back tomorrow."

Rosie wanted to skip down the aisle, but chose to do a fast walk instead. Carrie and Lauren ran up on either side of her. When they stepped out of the barn, Rosie caught her breath. A dusting of snow covered the ground.

"It's snowing!" Rosie tilted her head toward the sky. The large, fluffy flakes melted as they landed on her warm face. The way it was coming down, tomorrow they'd be able to put the sleigh runners on the carts and drive Treasure and Charley through the snow.

As they continued toward the house, Rosie glanced over her shoulder at the manger scene. She stopped suddenly. The doll they had used for the practices was wrapped in a blanket, lying in the manger. "Look at that!"

Everyone turned toward the manger.

Jessie smiled. "I put the doll there last night—after we finished the nativity."

"Not that. I mean on the ground." Rosie pointed.

"Mittens!" Carrie said. "How did you get out?"

"Jes—sie!" Julie frowned at her daughter.

Jessie shook her head. "I didn't let her out—honest! I tied that red ribbon around her neck, then I put her in the pen with the other animals."

The sheep was fast asleep on a pile of hay, her back resting against the manger.

Jessie started toward Mittens. "I'll put her back."

"No." Grandma rested her hand on Jessie's shoulder. "Let her stay there."

Rosie stared at the sheep lying beside the manger. She began to sing softly, "Away in a manger, no crib for a bed."

The others joined in.

> *The little Lord Jesus laid down His sweet head.*
>
> *The stars in the sky looked down where He lay.*
>
> *The little Lord Jesus, asleep on the hay.*

"For unto us a child is born, unto us a son is given: and the government shall be upon his shoulder: and his name shall be called Wonderful, Counsellor, The mighty God, The everlasting Father, The Prince of Peace."

—Isaiah 9:6

Discussion Questions and Activities

Suggested use: read a chapter, then discuss the corresponding questions as desired. Since **parts of the story may be revealed by the questions**, you shouldn't read them ahead of the chapter. Choose questions that are suitable for the reader's age, interest, and abilities.

Chapters 1 & 2

1. Several times at the auction, Grandma pointed out that they couldn't afford to do everything Rosie wanted to do, specifically her desire to buy the two cremello mares, a fancier cart, and brand-new sets of harness. Learning to use money wisely takes time and experience, but you can begin at a young age. How could Rosie— or you—learn to handle money responsibly?

2. The Amish choose to lead a simpler life without modern conveniences such as automobiles and electricity. What are some advantages and disadvantages of their lifestyle? If you became Amish, what would you miss the most from your current life?

3. Rosie tried to determine Rascal's age by examining his teeth. The saying, "Don't look a gift horse in the mouth" relates to this ability to tell a horse's age from his teeth. What do you think the expression means?

4. The cremello coat color is produced when a cream dilution gene acts on a chestnut-colored horse. To dilute something means to reduce its strength. One dilute gene with the chestnut color results in palomino (lighter), while two dilute genes and chestnut produce cremello (even lighter). Coat colors and markings in horses are a result of complicated genetic factors that researchers still don't fully understand (evidence of an awesome Creator!) How many horse coat colors can you name? Which is your favorite?

Chapter 3

5. For readers of the previous book, *Rejoice With Me*, do you think the decision made by the race coordinators to ban Rosie and Abigail from the next race was fair? If not, what would your solution have been?

6. The name, Immanuel, means God with us. Through Jesus, we are able to see God the Father. "He that hath seen me hath seen the Father." John 14:9

Even though we don't know all the details surrounding the birth of Christ, the most important aspect of the Christmas story is that God became flesh. It is hard to comprehend the enormity of the fact that God, the Creator of the universe, stepped into time and space to become one of His creatures. To get a small taste of that, imagine yourself creating a set of people and animals from play-doh or clay. Think about what it would be like if you could become one of those characters in the little world you created.

7. Did Mary ride a donkey from Nazareth to Bethlehem? What do you think? Can you draw what the scene might have looked like, as Jessie did?

8. Luke 2:6 states, "that, while they were there, the days were accomplished that she should be delivered."

That verse suggests that Mary and Joseph did not rush into Bethlehem the very night Jesus was born. Most of us do not know the Greek language, but there are study aids that can help us understand Scripture by providing definitions of the original Greek of the New Testament.

Strong's concordance is one of those tools and is available free online. The word that the KJV translates "were accomplished" is *pletho*, and it means "to fill or fulfill, especially with regard to time, to accomplish."

You can see the Greek words for Luke 2 from this web page:

http://biblehub.com/kjvs/luke/2.htm

Hover over a word or phrase on that page to see the Strong's number and definition. Click the word or phrase to view the full definition and other places in the Bible where the same word is used. You can use Strong's to look up other words in the Christmas story—or any passage you want to study in the Bible.

Chapter 4

9. Download the harness identification sheet from the book's web page, and locate the pieces of harness the book describes.

http://www.sonrisestable.com/books/sonrise-stable-book8-operation-christmas-spirit

10. After Rascal has been at the farm a while, it becomes obvious that he was not trained for harness and is, indeed, a mischief-maker. Rosie is surprised that the boy who sold Rascal lied about the pony. Can you find verses in the Bible that relate to being honest? Who is called the Father of Lies? Why is it important to tell the truth?

11. Can you find the Greek word translated "inn" in Luke 2:7 using a Strong's concordance? What does it mean? Do you think Mary and Joseph would have stayed in something like a hotel—or a spare room in the home of family or friends?

12. What is the Greek word for "manger"? Do you think Jesus was born in a stable? Or was it a cave, like Jessie was so excited about?

13. Rosie's idea for the live nativity at Sonrise Stable helped the kids keep their focus on the birth of Christ during the Christmas season. It would also bring other people to the stable so they could see the Biblical story. What are some things you can do to keep your focus on Christ during the holiday? Is there a way you can use this special time of year to witness to others?

Chapter 5

14. Rosie was a little frustrated with how much time it was taking to train the ponies. Why was it important to do things like leading

them around with the harness, then line driving before hooking them up to the carts?

15. The entire family was disappointed when Gabe did not come to live with them. Do you know a family that has foster children? If so can you think of any way you might be able to help them? There are thousands of children in foster care, and it can be challenging at times for both the children and the foster parents.

Chapter 6

16. Why do you think God chose to reveal the birth of Christ to shepherds first?

17. Billy told a humorous story about an experience he had at a young age with an ornery sheep. Sheep are not known for being the smartest animals.

Phillip Keller's book, *A Shepherd Looks at Psalm 23*, provides wonderful spiritual insights into the many references to sheep in the Bible. There is also a children's version, *A Child's Look at the 23rd Psalm*. See what you can discover about sheep using those or other references.

Why are sheep mentioned more times in the Bible than any other animal?

18. As Jessie's big brother, Jared tried to keep an eye on her when his parents weren't around. Although older siblings don't have the same role or authority as a parent, they do have an impact on younger siblings—for better or worse. Do you think Jared was a good older brother? What did he do well, and what could he have done better? If you have younger siblings, relatives, or friends, how can you be a positive role model for them?

19. What do you think about the children's decision not to receive gifts that Christmas?

20. Would you like to have your own Operation Christmas Spirit? Think of someone you could give a gift to who would not expect

to receive anything from you. You might even choose to give anonymously so they don't know who the gift was from.

21. Rosie was disappointed when she chose Abigail's name. Sometimes God calls us to do things that we don't find easy. Can you think of anything Rosie could give or do for Abigail?

22. Identify blinders on the pony harness (from the sheet mentioned in question 9). Not everyone uses blinders when driving. Do you think it would be better to use them or not? Read Hebrews 12:1-2. What should our focus be as we go through life?

Chapter 7

23. Many people who don't know much about horses think they are like a bicycle; you just get on them and go. But horses are not machines; they're animals with unique personalities. They learn at their own pace and respond differently in various situations. Compare Rascal and Charley's personalities and their responses to the training. Are you more like Rascal or Charley?

24. Have you ever wondered why God didn't provide more details in the Bible? Do you think when we reach heaven we'll instantly know everything? Or will we continue to learn there?

Chapter 8

25. Rosie was so excited when she was finally able to drive Rascal for the first time! Describe a time when you worked hard at, or waited for, something a long time. How did it feel while you were waiting?

26. Have you ever ridden in a horse or pony cart? Watch the cart video on the sonrisestable.com website.

http://www.sonrisestable.com/sonrise-stable-books-videos/

Moving at a slower speed and being in closer contact with nature makes horse-drawn transportation a lot different than riding in a car. What are the advantages and disadvantages of horse-drawn travel?

27. Rosie felt God prodding her to invite Abigail to the live nativity at Sonrise Stable. She knew it would be a good thing to do, but she didn't obey at first. God continued to prompt her, and she finally obeyed. Have you had a similar experience when you felt God asking you to do something? Did you obey immediately?

28. Rosie couldn't believe Jared wanted to ask Abigail to play the part of Mary. She didn't want Abigail to have the part. Who do you think was right—Jared or Rosie? Why?

Chapter 9

29. Do you have any idea why Billy and Sassy were pulling the log up to the barn?

30. Why did Rosie tell Abigail that Billy might be going to college? How did Rosie feel after she told the lie?

Chapter 10

31. Who do you think was shooting a gun in the woods at Sonrise Stable?

32. How did Rascal and Charley respond to the gunshots?

33. At first, what was Rosie more worried about than the pain in her side?

Chapter 11

34. Should Billy have gone out in the woods to find the hunter after Rosie's accident? Why or why not?

35. How would you feel if you were in Carrie's position after Billy left? Her aunt was supposed to be there soon, but for a short time, she would be alone at the farm.

36. How did Rosie feel when she learned what Billy had done? If you've read the earlier books in the series, you know that at first Rosie didn't like Billy. How have her feelings about him changed and why?

Chapter 12

37. After the accident, Rosie had to rest for several weeks. Have you ever been cooped up like that for a long time because of an illness or injury? What did Rosie decide to do to make wise use of that time? What other things might she have done? Read Ephesians 5:15-17 for some good advice about how we should use our time. How does Romans 8:28 apply to this situation also?

Chapter 13

38. Many people have the misconception that the wise men arrived with their gifts for baby Jesus when He was still in the manger at the stable. Where in Scripture is the story of the wise men? When approximately does it indicate the wise men arrived?

39. What do you think the star that guided the wise men was? Do you think it's possible that the star was the Shekinah glory of God?

40. Research more about what the gifts of gold, frankincense, and myrrh are and why they might have been given to Jesus.

Chapter 14

41. How did you feel about Rascal being sent back to the Amish farm? Do you think it was the right decision? Why do you think no one told Rosie about this right away?

42. Things didn't work out as Abigail had hoped with Billy and the nativity practice. Do you think she'll continue to play the part of Mary?

43. Do some research on donkeys. How do they differ from horses and mules in their personality and physical appearance?

Chapter 15

44. Have you ever attended a live nativity performance? Try to find one at a nearby church or farm. Perhaps you could volunteer to help or to play one of the parts.

45. Were you surprised that Abigail continued with her role as Mary? Why do you think she might have done that?

46. How did Billy feel after playing Joseph in the nativity?

47. Abigail participated in the live nativity, but it didn't affect her the same way it did Billy. Do you think Abigail may respond to the message later?

48. What do you think Jessie meant when she said Mittens gave some of her wool to baby Jesus?

Chapter 16

49. When Rosie discovered that Abigail's horse had been sold, she was unsure whether to still give her the gift she had made. Would you have given it to her?

50. Why does Abigail believe Rosie doesn't like her? How do you feel the family treated Abigail? Was there anything more they could have done to make her feel loved?

51. Why do you think Billy said that Sassy was on a diet?

Chapter 17

52. What would you do on Christmas Day if your family had a no-gifts Christmas?

53. What is a favorite gift or memory from your past Christmases?

54. Why did the recipients of the gifts find it unsettling to receive a gift when they had nothing to give in return? For example, Mrs. Wilson wanted to pay Jared for mowing her lawn.

55. Of the gifts given in this chapter, and Rosie's gift in the previous one, which was your favorite and why?

Chapter 18

56. Were you surprised that Jessie made a gift for everyone?

57. Make your own manger scene, as Jessie did, from popsicle sticks and a clothespin. Or use modeling clay to make a full nativity set.

58. Can you think of a small gift you could make for your friends or family?

59. Of all the gifts given, Jessie's gift of the truck for Billy was the only one that involved significant cost. Do you think it was the cost of the gift that mattered to Billy?

Chapter 19

60. How did you feel when Rosie discovered Abigail had thrown her gift in the trash? How would you have felt if you had made the gift?

61. Why do you think Abigail threw the gift away, while someone like Grandma treasured her handmade gift?

62. A loving father can help children have a better idea of what God, our heavenly Father, is like. How did Eric help Rosie feel better when her gift was rejected?

63. Although it was a painful lesson, what new understanding of God did Rosie gain from this experience?

The Sonrise Stable Series

Available at sonrisestable.com & amazon.com